WELSH RUGBY
What Went Wrong?

I Catrin, Dan a Lwsi

WELSH RUGBY

What Went Wrong?

SEIMON WILLIAMS

First impression: 2023

© Copyright Seimon Williams and Y Lolfa Cyf., 2023

The publishers wish to acknowledge
the support of the Books Council of Wales.

Cover design: Sion Ilar

ISBN: 978-1-912631-50-6

Published and printed in Wales
on paper from well-maintained forests by
Y Lolfa Cyf., Talybont, Ceredigion SY24 5HE
website www.ylolfa.com
e-mail ylolfa@ylolfa.com
tel 01970 832 304

Contents

Foreword
by Stephen Jones

THIS IS A book that had to be written, and congratulations to Seimon Williams for his hard work, the meticulous research and the clarity of his words. Frankly, what he has produced is a compelling and readable textbook on the long decline and the struggles of Welsh rugby – the heartbeat of the nation has become fainter.

Indeed, his may be one of the most important rugby books of the era. It will compel the reader – and yet I also hope that it enrages the reader as it has enraged me.

If it does, then Seimon Williams will have done rugby in Wales a wonderful service. *Welsh Rugby: What Went Wrong?* takes the story of the sport before professionalism, and right up through to the present day.

In passing, I should say that it seems absolutely typical that on the very day I am writing this Foreword, Wales are playing an utterly meaningless match against the Barbarians, therefore extending by yet another week the absence of players who were away for months and months preparing for and playing the Rugby World Cup in France.

Why would Welsh clubs bother developing international players when they scarcely ever see them again? That is an issue well discussed herein. Why does the WRU not realise that by their decades-long stance against proper treatment they could be on the point of killing the Welsh pro game?

Most of us who follow the sport – and more particularly the sport in Wales – are grimly used to the bungling of successive

WRU administrations, the continuing bickering between small clubs and big clubs, and big clubs and the union; a disastrous decline of once-proud major Welsh clubs who used to dominate fixtures with English clubs but who these days struggle to lift the skin off a rice pudding.

More and more. Here we read about the deceit of contacts with South Africa, the dreadful years without Grand Slams, when it seemed that Wales were ceasing to become a major rugby nation; the years of desertion to rugby league, the funereal pace at which the old guard WRU reformed itself, just because the old guard wanted to keep their posts and free trips.

And since the departure from the scene of the likes of Ray Williams and Gareth Davies and a tiny few others, the miserable failure of Welsh rugby to produce great administrators. My list is not exhaustive, but I'd be surprised if readers could name three more.

And more recently, the struggle of the smaller clubs and continuous postponements, the death of regular, weekend rugby matches played by schools; plus, the crowing of the Football Association of Wales that rugby is no longer the national sport of the country. The jury is out on that, and Seimon writes well on the issue, but it still must be a savage blow to all those of us who felt earlier in our lives that rugby's position was impregnable.

Then this is when you fall onto your knees to give thanks to people like Warren Gatland, Alun Wyn Jones, Dan Biggar, Ken Owens and so many other players of the recent generation. They deserved to play in fine teams but had to fight through some poor runs.

In my opinion, it is totally down to Gatland and the top players that Wales have been so competitive in so many World Cups. The rest of the sport in Wales did not deserve that.

But the triumph of Seimon Williams is that he has codified all the horror decisions, the useless administration, all the silly calls and self-interest and codified it all into one authoritative, powerfully-researched book which deserves to become seen as the history of years in which Welsh rugby has always teetered on the edge of disaster.

After reading *Welsh Rugby: What Went Wrong?* you will understand, you will know exactly why we are here.

The detail is excellent, and some people will surely be seething to work out how it came about that the Welsh teams first played in a Celtic League with which they had no previous affiliations, and are now in something called the URC, a weighty pan-continental event which will do very little for global warming and even less, you feel, for Welsh rugby.

Even now, I find it staggering that Welsh professional clubs are not playing in their natural environment – amongst the English professional clubs. It must happen, and happen soon.

And what of the near £90m windfall over five years which emanated from CVC, a shadowy investment company if there ever was one, and which bought up Wales in the Celtic rugby and the Six Nations?

The description by Seimon of it being effectively frittered away to background projects, rather than reinforcing the core of Welsh rugby in its professional guise, is amazing. We hear that a roof walk could be installed on the top of the Principality Stadium. How marvellous. Maybe it will be some kind of modern equivalent to walking the plank.

The Welsh Rugby Union is in the first footholds of recovery. The new look union has yet to prove itself. For us all to work out how not to do it, I refer you to this book. Who knows, by the time our anger subsides, we may be getting somewhere after a gap of over 30 years.

Stephen Jones
The Sunday Times

Introduction

ON 16 DECEMBER 1905, the New Zealand 'Originals' – the first fully representative New Zealand team to tour the northern hemisphere – rolled into Cardiff for the 28th match of their tour. They had won every single game, scoring 801 points and conceding just 22. Wales would be the last of the four international teams they would face and they had already comfortably seen off Scotland, England and Ireland.

Wales were no slouches, either. They had, earlier that year, completed a Triple Crown (which, in those days, before France let alone Italy had been admitted to the championship, meant a clean sweep). They hadn't lost a game in Cardiff in six years and were right in the middle of the first Golden Era of Welsh rugby. This was the team of Gwyn Nicholls, Percy Bush, Rhys Gabe and Dicky Owen.

Their meeting – between the best of the north and the best of the south – became known as the Match of the Century and still, nearly 120 years later, captures the imagination. In an almighty tussle, Teddy Morgan scored a try, Bob Deans was controversially disallowed an equalising score and Wales won 3–0.

But the match has a greater significance. For international sport in general and for Welsh nationhood in particular.

The band played 'Men of Harlech' as the players came on to the pitch. The New Zealanders performed the Haka. Wales had – officially – no response. How could they? There was no accepted ceremony for the beginning of international sporting tussles. However, in the weeks leading up to the game, some of the players had discussed whether they should respond, and how. A national conversation developed in Welsh newspapers, with the most popular of the options settling around adopting an existing song as an anthem.

And that's how the players found themselves singing 'Hen Wlad Fy Nhadau' back at the New Zealand team. And the crowd – having followed the debate in the newspapers – joined in. And, it is often claimed, this became the first instance of a national anthem being sung before an international sporting contest.

From that day, rugby and the nation of Wales became inextricably linked.

A Wales which then had no government of its own. A Wales which had no political or legal status. A Wales which did not even have a firmly defined border. A Wales which existed, to all intents and purposes, in the hearts and minds and in the languages and cultures of its people.

And on the international rugby field.

After all, as Eric Hobsbawm suggested, 'the imagined community of millions seems more real as a team of eleven (or fifteen) named people.'[1]

Rugby became 'absorbed into the Welsh self-image'.[2] As George Ewart Evans wrote in *The Strength of the Hills*: 'No one can understand the seriousness that is paid to rugby in Wales unless he views it as a social and political affirmation of its nationhood. For a nation that has existed for many years as a subject to a more powerful one, it is the sheet-anchor of its self-respect.'[3]

Many of the generations which followed expressed their Welshness through the rugby team. And not just the national team. When Warren Gatland was first courted by the WRU in 2007, it is said that one of the key factors in his decision to accept the job was a helicopter ride taken with the then WRU chief executive Roger Lewis. Within a single hour-long swoop above the central valleys of south Wales, it became clear to Gatland that this was rugby country. Countless pairs of rugby posts bookended endless green rectangles, village after village, town after town, valley after valley.

Rugby is a niche sport played to a good level in a handful of countries. It can lay claim to being the national sport of New Zealand. Some of the islands of the Pacific, too, either in its full form or in the shorter Sevens version.

And Wales?

In the years since the national men's football team started reappearing in the finals of major tournaments, the debate about which of rugby or football is the national sport has re-ignited.

In terms of participation numbers – both playing and physically attending as spectators at sub-national level – football is by some distance more popular. Welsh rugby sometimes stands accused of insularity, an assertion which has some legs. The disappearance of the old rugby songs hasn't been countered with the emergence of new ones – to the extent that it could be said, as the historian Gareth Williams has, that in Wales 'rugby football retains the image – by now a cliché and often a caricature – it acquired in the early years of the twentieth century'.[4]

The current affairs website nation.cymru carried an article ahead of a major qualifying match for the 2018 FIFA World Cup entitled 'Win or lose today, Welsh football has shown rugby what a national sport looks like'. Its author, Ifan Morgan Jones – while confessing that he is primarily a rugby supporter – commented that 'when it comes to building a national team, the Welsh FA is showing the WRU how it's done. It has little to do with anything happening on the pitch and everything to do with culture, attitude and national pride surrounding the team.'[5]

There is something in this, but much of the comparison between Welsh rugby and football is a little overblown.

Yes, Prince William is patron of the WRU, but his grandmother was patron of the FAW. Wales rugby coach

Warren Gatland received an OBE in 2014 for services to the game in this country, just as Chris Coleman received an OBE after Euro 2016. The FAW publishes its annual report bilingually, as does the WRU. Both run partially bilingual websites, in that not everything on the 'full' English version appears on the Welsh version. The national football team conducts parts of its press conferences in Welsh, with players taking questions in the language, as does the national rugby team. Yr Orsedd has previously honoured the likes of Gareth Edwards and Grav, just as it has Osian Roberts and Ian Gwyn Hughes.

More significantly, the Football Association of Wales and the national football team have managed to portray themselves as modern, outward-looking, fiercely patriotic and very much not part of the Welsh or British Establishment. The national men's football team and its governing body are now held up – as that nation.cymru piece suggests – as an example of a new, vibrant and modern Welsh sensibility.

In 2023, the game of rugby is in danger of losing its hold on the Welsh imagination. Yes, the national stadium continues to sell out for Six Nations games and whenever the All Blacks are in town. And, on those rare occasions a Welsh professional team is competitive at the top of the United Rugby Championship (URC) in its various iterations and in European competition, the crowds are there. But on the whole the days of bumper crowds in domestic rugby are long gone. In the immediate post-war period, Leicester – one of the great historic clubs of English rugby – drew an aggregate crowd across the 1949–50 season of 21,000. Cardiff drew twice that number to one game, a year later, when they faced Newport at the Arms Park in front of 48,500. That attendance wasn't a one-off, either. Forty thousand watched Swansea v Cardiff in 1952 and while crowds declined throughout the 1950s, it was still possible to attract over 30,000 to Cardiff v Newport games in both towns in 1955–56 and 35,000 for

Cardiff v Llanelli in 1958. By the late 1990s, crowds for elite club games were down to four figures and sometimes even three. Attendances recovered in the early regional era but are now heading south again.

Many people who did not already have an affiliation with one of the founder clubs of the post-2003 regions have not shifted their allegiances, although others clearly have. A 'domestic' league which involves four Welsh teams struggling to compete with vastly better resourced Irish, South African, Scottish and even Italian teams, doesn't attract the casual supporter. Games are spread across the weekend and the season so that there is no rhythm or regularity. Professional teams are denuded of their best players for half the season and that's on the assumption that, when they return from Wales duty, they are not injured and unfit to play.

Welsh rugby has been beset by incessant bickering. The fortunes of the national and professional teams have declined. At the same time, the Welsh Rugby Union has seemed to become ever more firmly entrenched within the Establishment. It has appeared complacent, as though it is an organisation which tinkers rather than strategizes, all the while worrying the carcase of an old song.

Then-chairman David Pickering had to apologise for using WRU facilities to arrange Labour Party events in the 2010s. The union has been criticised many times for its attitude towards the Welsh language. Match-day at the Principality Stadium (named for the building society which sponsors it, not as an ill-informed reference to Wales' constitutional status) often has a (British) military theme.

The South African writer Donald McRae wrote, in *Winter Colours*, of the Wales v New Zealand match in 1953. The radio coverage in New Zealand started ten minutes early, with no commentary, so that listeners back home could hear the singing in Cardiff. That singing – for so long uniquely identified with the Arms Park – has all but disappeared and you're lucky to

13

get the chorus only (often with the wrong words) of two songs in 2023.

If this millennium has seen the game in Wales in trouble, the early 2020s have pushed the accelerator on the process. The Coronavirus pandemic blew a hole in the game's finances from which it has yet to recover. The result is a mess of underfunding, of thwarted agreements, of uncertainty for players and supporters. Worse still, revelations in early 2023 about the culture at the WRU – of tales of sexism and misogyny and bullying and homophobia and racism and of the inability or unwillingness of the WRU board and its executive to tackle these issues – point to an organisation in serious trouble.

But how did we get here? How did a game which has meant so much to the people of Wales reach the point of endless crisis? Much of this is about the governance of the game and the way in which Welsh rugby stumbled from its amateur past into the professional era. The WRU is now a nearly £100m-a-year business, but it is still largely run by structures which – although amended and altered from time to time – echo those lost days of amateurism.

It is sometimes said that those who don't learn from history are doomed to repeat it. This book is an attempt to understand the history of rugby in Wales over the past 40 years in the hope that, once recognised, we will not.

November 2023

CHAPTER 1

Decline and Fall

'Welsh rugby, walking tall, crossed the threshold
of its second century. On the way in, it managed
simultaneously to graze its head and stub its toe.
The next twenty years would see it flailing to stay
upright, when it was not flat on its face.'[1]

(Dai Smith and Gareth Williams, 'Beyond the Fields of
Praise: Welsh Rugby 1980–1999', in Richards, H.,
Stead, P. and Williams, G., *More Heart and Soul*)

AS WELSH RUGBY entered its second century, it was – or, at
least, believed itself to be – in rude health.

The 1980–81 season would cement the country's place at
the forefront of the world game. The Welsh Rugby Union's
centenary celebrations had set itself the ambition of 'making a
significant contribution to rugby knowledge and thinking'.[2] It
had invited 150 delegates from 47 countries to attend a world
conference for coaches and referees.

Wales would show itself off to the world.

The union's self-regard at that point in time was not entirely
misplaced. The previous decade had been one of unparalleled
success for the national team. In ten completed Five Nations
championships between 1969 and 1979 (the 1972 edition
remained incomplete as security concerns prevented Wales
and Scotland from travelling to Dublin), Wales finished top

(either solely or jointly) eight times, winning six Triple Crowns and three Grand Slams. They had supplied the bulk of the Lions squads throughout the decade and two of its three head coaches.

The one missing element was a victory over the All Blacks.

There had been several narrow – not to mention controversial – misses during the 1970s. No matter. The crowning achievement of the Crowning Years would be to beat the 1980 All Blacks and confirm Wales' place at the top of the world game.

The celebratory Test match was a disaster. New Zealand strolled to a 23–3 victory. It was Wales' heaviest home defeat in 98 years.

A middling Five Nations in 1981 gave way to an encouraging victory over the touring Australians later that year.

The 1982 championship ended in ignominy, Scotland running up their highest points total in the fixture since 1924 in condemning Wales to a first home Five Nations defeat in 14 years and 27 games. They finished bottom of the pile, wooden spoonists for the first time since 1967. Seven players were summarily dropped – five of whom never played for Wales again.

The following year, the WRU awarded caps for a match against a non-founder member of the International Rugby Board for the first time. Romania thanked the WRU for the honour by running riot in Bucharest in a four tries to nil, 24–6 thrashing. It was Wales' heaviest away defeat in 14 years. The 1984 Wallabies played some glorious rugby in winning all four Tests in Britain and Ireland, but they were fallible – falling to defeats against Cardiff, Llanelli, South of Scotland and Ulster. The 28–9 thrashing administered to Wales was made all the worse by the sight of an Australian eight shoving their Welsh counterparts all around the pitch, culminating in the humiliation of a pushover try.

Coaches and players came and went in a period of increasing instability.

Times of uncertainty within the Welsh game, often coupled with economic stress, had historically led to an exodus of talent to the paid ranks of rugby league. Rugby union was, after all, still an amateur game. In the league code, players could receive payments for training and playing. It was this practice which had caused the split between the two codes in 1895. Such was the enmity between the codes that Martin Johnes recalled: 'As the proverb went, there were three things best not discussed in polite Welsh society: politics, religion and rugby league.'³

Receiving payment for playing, taking part in a trial for a rugby league club, even daring to speak to a rugby league scout, would be enough to have a player banned *sine die*. Former players weren't safe in retirement either, as Adrian Smith wrote: 'A ghosted biography, a place in the commentary box, or a column in the *Western Mail* meant no further involvement in the game at any level, whether in coaching or administration.'⁴

Even so, ways were found to make life a little easier for the top players. The young Barry John would occasionally receive the proceeds of a whip-round among the spectators at his games. Others might be presented with a bundle of cash for wearing the boots of a particular manufacturer. Others still found brown envelopes stuffed with notes in their boots after a game. Some of the grander clubs, such as Cardiff, would not countenance such flagrant abuses of the rules, but would find their players jobs with local firms which provided company cars, clothing, meals and a solid career path for their post-rugby lives.

The game's burgeoning profile meant that Five Nations matches became staples of winter afternoon television schedules from the 1960s. *Rugby Special* arrived in 1966 with the first regular package of highlights. With eyeballs on the sport, advertising crept in. And so, the push towards professionalisation began. But it would not come from within the game's administration.

Where cricket went in the late 1970s, David Lord – an Australian entrepreneur – tried to take rugby union in 1983. World Series Cricket was loud, garish and colourful. Lord had the idea of a rugby circus along similar lines. Approaches were made to over 200 of the world's best players. Leading Welsh players were tempted, but the deal was both secret and speculative. Lord accused Wales hooker Bobby Windsor of having spilled the beans, at which point the whole show quickly fell apart.[5]

In France, meanwhile, amateurism was little more than a charade. Former Wales fly-half Gareth Davies takes up the story: 'I captained the Baabaas against Australia in the last game of the [1984] tour. I roomed with Jérôme Gallion, the scrum-half. Fantastic player. He was playing for Toulon at the time. He asked me if I wanted to go to play for Toulon. The club president's daughter phoned me the next day, just to say that she'd been speaking to Jérôme... they offered me £24,000 a year, an apartment and a job with the local authority if I wanted it, a car and so on. It was pretty tempting, much more than I was earning at the time. But it was just the fact that it was so uncertain. It was obviously an under-the-table sort of deal anyway, so if you got injured you'd be on the scrapheap. I had a job, so I bottled it really. I didn't really regret it, but I sometimes regret that I didn't get the opportunity to do it, as the boys do now.'[6]

The national team trod water for the next few years, losing both home championship games in 1984 for the first time in 21 years, but winning both away games. Notable victories and dispiriting defeats arrived in equal measure.

The decline in the fortunes of the national team didn't tally, for many, with the perceived strength of the club game. Clubs including Bridgend, Cardiff, Llanelli and Swansea were among those who beat touring international teams in the 1980s and early 1990s. Pontypool and London Welsh were multiple champions of the unofficial Anglo-Welsh leagues maintained by various publications, from the 1960s to the 1980s, while Bridgend, Swansea and Newport were among other Welsh clubs to triumph.

Gareth Davies concurs: 'You could argue that the club structure in the 1980s was stronger than in the 1970s. In the '70s you had a lot of strong teams. You could never bank on a win – you went to the Gnoll, or to the Talbot Athletic, everybody was competitive. But then in the 1980s it was even more competitive. You had Pontypool at the forefront, Pontypridd, so the teams we were playing with Cardiff at the time, I felt I was up against quality, international class outside-halves. You had Paul Turner, Stuart Lewis at Pontypridd, Peter Davies at Neath, Gary Pearce at Llanelli. Every team had a good scrum-half too. There was real strength in depth, in every position. You were always up against some nutter of a number 7. So, I don't think the performances of the Wales team on the field in the 1980s reflected the strength of the club game.'[7]

The inaugural Rugby World Cup, to be held in 1987 in New Zealand and Australia, would provide a marker of Wales' current standing. It would also open a few eyes to the increasing professionalism of the southern hemisphere.

'I remember Ray Williams [then WRU secretary] coming round before the first game,' Jonathan Davies, then the national team's fly-half and talisman, recalled in a recent S4C documentary: 'We were watching New Zealand against Italy – and he said, "Right boys, you need to sign these forms now to say that you won't make money out of the game for the next six months." So we all signed because we knew no different. Next thing, before the game started, John Kirwan came on in an advert on television. And I remember thinking, "We've just signed these forms and here's a boy playing on the wing for New Zealand in this game in five minutes, and he's in an advert on television!"'[8]

Wales won five of their six games – breezing past Ireland and England and recording a thrilling last-minute win over

Australia in the process – but the sole defeat was a crushing 49–6 loss to New Zealand in the semi-finals. Team manager Clive Rowlands brushed off the massacre, explaining to journalists that Wales would simply go back to beating England.

Wales indeed did just that in 1988, beating England first up, squeezing past Scotland courtesy of two of the tries of the decade from Jonathan Davies and Ieuan Evans, before clinching a first Triple Crown in nine years in Dublin. The Grand Slam game against France in Cardiff was a step too far, ending in a 10–9 defeat for a share of the title. That win over Ireland proved to be the last time Wales would achieve two consecutive victories in championship matches for six years.

Returning to New Zealand in the summer of 1988 as Five Nations champions, the yawning chasm between the best of the south and the best of the north became ever more apparent. The itinerary for the tour was brutal, with New Zealand coach Alex Wylie stating that he would never have accepted it for his team. The accommodation was awful – hotels were so cold that some players took to sleeping in their tour tracksuits, one of the hotels was situated next to a sawmill – and the provincial game defeats and injuries piled up. The two Tests were lost by record scores – 52–3 and 54–9.

Whitbread Rugby World '89 reported that 'cynics in New Zealand reckoned [Wales] would be about the third best team in the South Island of New Zealand and about sixth best in the North Island… not counting the Maori or the All Blacks' 1st, 2nd or even 3rd XV.'[9]

Jonathan Davies and other senior players asked for permission to address the WRU's general committee on their return. Their request was refused.

'If you go on a trip to somewhere like New Zealand,' said Davies, 'if you don't learn something from that, you'll learn nothing, because at the time they were the best. But they [the WRU] just said, "Look, we make the decisions, you're players and the game is amateur," and that's all we heard. Nothing changed.'[10]

So, what did the Welsh Rugby Union do to arrest the decline? Its first instinct was to blame the coaches of the national team. Tony Gray – despite leading his country to third place at the World Cup and a Triple Crown – was relieved of his duties.

Beyond the rugby field, Wales was hit hard by the decline of heavy industry. In 1980, there were still 27,000 mineworkers working 36 pits across south Wales, but by 1990 there was only one pit left. In the Rhondda, where there were once 50,000 working miners, the entire population of the area had declined to around that figure. The steel and tinplate industries – so important to the western and eastern extremities of the south Wales rugby belt – were, by 1990, a third of their 1979 size.

'As it entered the 1990s, therefore,' wrote Smith and Williams, 'Wales was a very different place from what it had been in the 1960s and 1970s, let alone an earlier period. The last two decades of the twentieth century saw Wales undergo a dramatic transformation and no part of society – politics, culture, education, or sport – was unaffected by it.'[11]

During the economic crisis of the 1920s and 1930s, 69 capped Welsh players left Wales for rugby league clubs in the north of England. The game in the country went into a tailspin – the national team won just nine games from 32 played between 1923 and 1930.

'Lack of success was cause and effect of selectorial myopia and administrative inadequacy. Tactical bankruptcy on the field reflected financial insolvency off it,'[12] wrote Gareth Williams.

By the 1980s, these economic pressures, combined with the struggles of the national team on the field and frustration at the inertia of both the International Rugby Board and the Welsh Rugby Union, again made the game in Wales vulnerable to that apex predator of twentieth-century sport, the rugby league scout.

Players started to look north once more. Between 1985 and 1989, Terry Holmes, Stuart Evans, Robert Ackerman, Gary Pearce, Adrian Hadley, David Bishop, Paul Moriarty, John Devereux and Jonathan Griffiths were among those to leave for rugby league.

With the 1989 Five Nations looming and a Lions tour to follow at the end of the season, Jonathan Davies' departure for Widnes early in the new year prompted a period of national mourning. Davies was a certainty for the Lions, very likely as captain, but even that carrot was not enough to keep him in rugby union. Invited to contribute to the S4C coverage of the Wales v England game at the end of the championship, Davies wasn't allowed into the stadium to work, with WRU secretary David East arguing that giving him entry would be permitting him to promote 'non-amateur rugby'. Davies eventually gave his pre-match comments, surrounded by dozens of supporters, on Canton Bridge, a few hundred yards from the stadium. The WRU's actions were condemned by MPs the following week. Davies himself came close to suing the WRU for restraint of trade, stating – understandably – that the press box was full of ex-players who had 'professionalised' themselves by taking up careers in which they spoke or wrote about the game they had once played. He remained furious with all the unions of these islands for their stance on amateurism: 'I can't see the powers in British rugby relenting, because it is not so much amateurism they are trying to preserve, they are preserving themselves.'[13]

Wales' contribution to the 1989 Lions tour was much reduced compared to the previous decade. Only seven players made the initial selection, but several – notably Robert Jones, David Young and Ieuan Evans – made significant interventions in securing the Lions' first series victory since 1974.

The tour had been the Lions' first in six years. The 1986 tour should have visited South Africa, but the rugby community had belatedly noticed that maintaining relationships with an apartheid state was perhaps unwise. As such, South Africa had been ostracised from the international rugby family during the 1970s and 1980s. 'Ostracised from the international rugby family', in this context, appears to have meant receiving Lions tours in 1974 and 1980 and official visits from New Zealand (1976), Ireland (1981), France (1983) and England (1984). There were also non-Test-status tours by the South American Jaguares (1980 and 1982) and the New Zealand Cavaliers (1986). And the South African Rugby Board (SARB) retained full voting membership of the International Rugby Board. But they were barred from the first two Rugby World Cups in 1987 and 1991 and were unable to tour any of the nations of Britain and Ireland nor New Zealand from 1970, Australia after 1971 and France after 1974.

The Welsh Rugby Union, while it did not receive the Springboks after 1970 and did not send an official Wales team to South Africa after 1964, 'seemed to obliterate more profound areas of its moral consciousness in blind pursuit of sporting entertainment'[14] according to the historian K.O. Morgan. It accepted a multi-racial South African Barbarians team in 1979 – drawn from three entirely separate, racially-segregated South African unions in the form of SARB, SARFF and SARA/SARU, all of which provided eight players each. The team played two of its seven matches in Wales. Cardiff City Council protested, eventually withdrawing its support for the WRU's centenary celebrations the following year.

At the WRU AGM in 1984, its constituent clubs decided by a 306 to 62 mandate to maintain links with SARB. The WRU then tolerated a tour of South Africa by the Crawshays invitational team – featuring five Lions and five further then-current Welsh internationals – the following year.

To celebrate its centenary, SARB hoped to persuade the Lions – on their way home from that successful tour of

Australia – to play a number of matches in South Africa. The Lions refused. SARB instead issued invitations to the major unions, asking them to forward the invitations to players and administrators in an attempt to put together a World XV.

The WRU did so. In total, ten Welsh players and six administrators made the trip in August 1989.

The tour was condemned back in Wales. At a fractious AGM in October 1989, the WRU's clubs voted by 276 to 113 to reverse its 1984 decision and to sever all rugby links with South Africa. An inquiry into the tour was established under the leadership of Vernon Pugh.

With the All Blacks due to visit Wales for the first time in nine years, warm-up games with Welsh clubs were arranged to allow the national team to develop its patterns. Wales managed to lose to a Bridgend team shorn of its internationals.

They were much improved in the return fixture with New Zealand but still fell to another record home defeat, this time by 34 points to 9. The 1990 Five Nations championship saw Wales' then-heaviest ever defeat to England by 34–6. John Ryan, brought in just 18 months earlier to replace Tony Gray, resigned.

Ron Waldron left Neath to replace Ryan and was given unprecedented power as the first Wales team manager, responsible for all Welsh representative men's teams from the senior team down to the Under-19s. The 'Big Five' selection panel was replaced by a three-man selection committee headed by Waldron, with David Richards (the only member of the Big Five to survive) and former coach Tony Gray. It wasn't enough to avoid Wales' first-ever championship whitewash. Neither was Waldron's transfer of Neath's all-action style able to prevent a series of catastrophic defeats.

The *Western Mail's* John Billot referred to the 1989–90 season as 'the most turbulent and humiliating season in the history of the WRU'[15] – those brave souls who make it to the end of this book may beg to differ with Billot's view – as recriminations mounted, mainly over the South Africa affair. Clive Rowlands resigned as WRU president but was later persuaded back. R.H. Williams, a national selector who had been expected to succeed Rowlands as president, withdrew when it became clear that he had publicly denied involvement in the tour while knowing that his travel arrangements had already been made. The WRU secretary David East had been in post for only eight months but, understanding that others had not been truthful with him about their involvement, resigned. On the field, the haemorrhaging of talent continued. The departures of David Young and Rowland Phillips meant that a third of 1988's Triple Crown team had gone. Later that year, Allan Bateman and Kevin Ellis – two new talents around whom a new team could have been built – also left for rugby league

The WRU tried to get back to the day job by publishing a 106-page review of the structure of Welsh rugby in 1990. The 78 initiatives included within a 'Quest for Excellence' had mostly already been identified in previous reviews but had been 'allowed to gather dust before being finally shredded as space was made for a new document'.[16] However, in an echo of debates which have raged ever since, it also proposed a complete remodelling of the administration of the game, from the appointment of a management board headed by a chief executive, to the replacement of districts with provincial-style unions.

In 2023, the districts endure.

Among the cures which had been identified for the ills of Welsh rugby was the proposed establishment of leagues.

On 6 October, the *Western Mail* reported that the governing body considered it 'desirable that a Welsh club championship be established, to consist of a first division, a second division and two district divisions, to be called the eastern and western divisions. The first division [will] consist of no more than ten clubs, it being insisted that the first teams of Cardiff, Swansea,

Newport and Llanelli should always form the nucleus of this division.' There would be promotion and relegation to and from the top-flight, with promotion in part governed by criteria, including the suitability of stadia.[17]

That's 6 October 1908. So long ago that the WRU was still known as the Welsh Football Union. The self-proclaimed first-class clubs would have none of it and insisted on arranging their own fixture lists, many of which included regular cross-border skirmishes with English clubs.

By 1975, national coaching coordinator Ray Williams started to push again for a formal league structure, later writing that: 'The structure that we have at the moment must be changed. It is largely an accident of history and is certainly not durable enough to sustain the game in Wales in the years to come. Success goes to those who plan properly.'[18]

The establishment of England's Courage League in 1987 both accelerated the development of the game in that country and reduced the opportunities for Welsh clubs to measure themselves against their traditional cross-border rivals. When those traditional games did take place, English clubs began to gain the upper hand. It was a far cry from Welsh domination a few years earlier – Terry Holmes recalled in his autobiography that he had faced English clubs 55 times for Cardiff and had lost only twice.[19]

Cardiff, Swansea and Llanelli were by now in favour of leagues but, disillusioned by the WRU's chaotic attempts at making the case in 1989, they withdrew their support. Eventually, the WRU were given a mandate by their member clubs to form a 38-team national league in four divisions. Wales would, finally, have a formal league structure for the 1990–91 season.

The decision was not universally welcomed. At Pontypool, Graham Price lamented that the WRU had previously kept out of 'meddling... the clubs organised the championship and merit table fixtures. It was successful, relevant and very meaningful.' Alun Carter went on to criticise the WRU's 'worrying blindness to the importance of traditional fixtures and regional networking... on the community level, people began to get out of the habit of watching rugby games and regarding them as major social occasions... the process of unpicking the club fabric had already been set in motion, one thread at a time.'[20]

It is perhaps unsurprising that the rugby people of the Gwent valleys were sceptical about the introduction of leagues. After all, between 1919 and 1990, Pontypool had won the unofficial Welsh championship nine times, a figure matched only by Cardiff. Neath with eight titles, Newport with seven, Llanelli with six and Aberavon and Bridgend with five each were other serial winners.

The humiliations continued. Saved from a second consecutive whitewash in 1991 by a fortuitous draw at home to Ireland, the national team nevertheless conceded 100 points in the Championship for the first time, their minus 72 points difference a full 52 points worse than that of the similarly winless Ireland. They were again on the end of a record defeat, this time their then-worst ever to France by 36–3. Scotland completed a first hat-trick of victories over Wales for nearly 70 years in 1991, England repeated the feat a year later.

Former Wales and Lions captain and coach John Dawes identified the root cause – 'we are light years behind in fitness, strength and determination... we have been overtaken'.[21]

As if to prove Dawes' point, and in a metaphor so unsubtle it might as well have come in the shape of a sledgehammer, New South Wales demolished poor old Wales 71–8 on the 1991 tour of Australia. The margin of defeat was slightly smaller in the following week's Test, but only because the Australian fly-half Michael Lynagh missed half of his twelve conversion attempts in a 63–6 reverse.

The Wales squad at least left their mark on Australia by brawling amongst themselves at the after-match dinner.

Billot's assertion that the 1989–90 season had been 'the most turbulent and humiliating season in the history of the WRU' had lasted all of a year. The cover of the following year's edition of the *Welsh Brewers' Rugby Annual for Wales* was a departure from tradition: 'The unique black border around the cover of this [edition] says it all,' wrote its editor, Arwyn Owen. 'Welsh rugby at senior international level is dead. It had been in extremely poor health for several seasons. However, the recent tour of Australia proved to be fatal.' Indeed, John Kennedy of the *Western Mail* wrote, in the same edition, that 'this was the day Welsh rugby died of shame'.[22]

So, things were bad. Very bad. Surely, they couldn't get any worse?

Of course they could.

The squad came home to prepare for the second Rugby World Cup. Waldron resigned through ill-health weeks before the tournament, to be replaced as head coach by Alan Davies.

Although the first and last matches of the 1991 Rugby World Cup was hosted by England, the type of horse-trading in which the rugby committeeman revels had seen an agreement reached to share matches among all Five Nations. Handily, all Wales' pool matches would be played in Cardiff. It didn't help. They lost to Western Samoa for the first time and suffered yet another record home defeat by 38 points to 3 against Australia, becoming the first of the IRB founder members to fail to progress beyond the pool stages.

With various coaches hired and then fired and a league system now in place to correct the weakening of the domestic game, Welsh rugby took the opportunity to indulge in a bit of good old-fashioned internecine warfare.

A special general meeting, called by the clubs for April 1993 following the leaking of the Vernon Pugh report into the 1989 South Africa tour (presented to the WRU in 1991 but never formally shared with the clubs), saw a vote of no confidence carried in the entire WRU general committee. Every member of the committee immediately left. The meeting carried on for a further three hours without them, during which three officials were asked to take charge while new elections were arranged. In typical fashion, the three did not see eye to eye. The resulting fall-out saw the issuing of writs and injunctions which cost the WRU over £40,000.

Pugh's inquiry attempted to gather information from those involved but found that: 'the attitude of the players to the union bordered on the contemptuous. That the union as a body, and particularly its committee structure, was an anachronism perpetuated for the benefit of its members. It was too large, too inexpert, unnecessary and out of place in the modern world. The players were hostile to the enquiry process and thought that it was a sham which involved a power struggle between different sections of the union.'[23]

It was little wonder that the players were contemptuous. Mike Hall recalled that, 'the committee sat at the front of the plane ordering champagne on the way to away internationals, while the players sat at the back. You would have an open bar for the whole period you were in Edinburgh or London or Dublin for the committee to get their noses in the trough, while the players would be charged for tea or coffee in their room. That attitude contributed to boys going to rugby league.'[24]

What's more, as the Pugh inquiry had suspected but could not prove, players and administrators had been paid handsomely for their South African trip. Despite 'running up against a wall of rehearsed answers and uncooperative witnesses',[25] Pugh concluded that on the balance of probabilities, at least one player had received more than £30,000 for a few weeks' work. Indeed, long after retiring, Mike Hall admitted to receiving many times more than his annual (then junior) surveyor's salary of £7,500 for his involvement. 'They knew we were paid, but brushed it under the carpet,'[26] he wrote later.

The broader conclusions of the Pugh report make for

sobering reading some 30 years on. It found that the WRU was a mess. Its administrative structure needed a wholesale overhaul, that an out-of-control proliferation of committees had led to self-interest and 'petty empire-building'; that a central executive of professional officers needed to be appointed based on talent and not on rote and that all of this, taken together, had created an organisation which tolerated behaviour which would be considered utterly unacceptable in any other comparable organisation.[27]

Some of the more enlightened elements within the northern hemisphere unions had identified potential loopholes in the regulations which could allow the leading players to make some kind of living from their profiles. Public relations jobs weren't, strictly speaking, against the rules. Gavin Hastings and Will Carling were two who effectively branded themselves as PR companies, Carling later admitting to having attained millionaire status and acknowledging that 'every penny I make is down to who I am and what I have achieved in the game'.[28] A handful of leading Welsh players, including most of the 1993 Lions, set up their own firm, Just Players, into which fees for public appearances could be deposited. It quickly started turning over £100,000 plus a year, almost all of which went directly to the still-amateur players. At Cardiff, Peter Thomas looked at investing a significant sum into the Athletic Club's rugby section with the intention of establishing trust funds for the players.[29] All – arguably – within the letter, if not the spirit, of the law. As Johnes wrote, 'amateurism in rugby became not a question of if you were paid but rather of how you were paid'.[30]

Nevertheless, in the north, the money which could legitimately be made by union players paled in comparison with the money available to their peers – both former union players who were now playing rugby league in the north of England and union players in the southern hemisphere. The

South African captain Francois Pienaar was said to be earning the equivalent of £200,000 a year as an amateur player. The flood of players moving to rugby league may have subsided, but the very best players were still targeted. One such player was Scott Gibbs. The sensation of the ultimately unsuccessful 1993 Lions tour to New Zealand, he had suffered a serious injury in the autumn 1993 Barbarians v New Zealand game and, during his time away, began to consider his options.

His club, Swansea, had striven pretty much every sinew, within the laws of the game, to put together a package to persuade him to stay. A combination of work and paid study worth around £35,000 at St Helen's, Swansea, couldn't compete with a package said to be worth many multiples more at St Helens in northern England. Unlike many of his predecessors, he did not leave with the – admittedly often begrudging – best wishes of his former club. Called a 'rugby prostitute' by Swansea, Gibbs railed at the hypocrisy: 'It grates me that I am called a prostitute while players and officials keep on covering up what's going on in union. Every player in Wales knows that when you play on a Saturday, if you win you can get a few quid. Players get the cash after the game.'[31]

The fortunes of the national team continued to fluctuate wildly. A solid 1992 saw two wins. A euphoric opening weekend victory over England in 1993 proved to be a mere prelude to three chastening defeats. A championship winning performance in 1994 presaged not a new dawn, but another whitewash in 1995. For the second successive World Cup, Wales dismissed the national team's leadership group weeks before the tournament. Alan Davies was no longer head coach, Ieuan Evans no longer captain. A Cardiff ticket of Alec Evans and his club captain Mike Hall would take Wales into the tournament. It was a disaster. A routine win first up against Japan was followed by a midweek game against a new

New Zealand team playing a more expansive brand of rugby. Among the All Blacks' weapons was an 18-stone, six-foot-five winger called Jonah Lomu. Wales team manager Geoff Evans declared that his team was bigger, better, faster and fitter that the All Blacks. They lost 34–9. The final game, against Ireland, is often rated among the worst international matches ever to be televised. Both teams were awful, Ireland marginally less so and Wales' World Cup was over in nine days.

But Wales' tribulations were small beer in comparison with the seismic developments in the southern hemisphere. Once again, rugby league was the root cause. Rumours were swirling that up to eleven All Blacks were ready to sign for the rival code, now awash with cash following a major television deal signed with Rupert Murdoch's Fox network.

Australian associates of Kerry Packer started to explore the potential for a breakaway rugby union competition, away from union control, in which television – Packer's television company – would rule.

The World Rugby Corporation would be a worldwide event, with a smaller number of high-quality domestic teams playing fewer, but better, matches. There would be teams in South Africa, Australia and New Zealand. There would also be teams in Europe. In Wales, that meant two teams, located in the two major population centres, Swansea and Cardiff.

Six weeks before the Rugby World Cup, Hall joined a meeting with Alec Evans and others. Hall was offered a $200,000 playing contract and a further $250,000 to sign up as many Welsh players as he could.

Murdoch's Fox then signed a $550m ten-year agreement with the unions of New Zealand, Australia and South Africa. The unions now had the money but not – yet – the players.

Discussions continued throughout that summer. Hall claimed that he had signed up 50 leading Welsh players, including every member of the national squad with the sole exception of his predecessor as national captain, Ieuan Evans.

The contracts were signed and held in escrow, ready to be triggered once World Rugby Corporation was ready to go public.

The WRU, dimly aware of these moves and in what was becoming a trademark locking-the-stable-door-after-the-horse-has-bolted gambit, issued a 23-point argument for the benefits of amateurism in July 1995. There wouldn't be enough money for ground and clubhouse maintenance if the game were to professionalise, they argued. Only the wealthiest clubs could survive. Players' agents would proliferate, each taking their cut and draining the game of money.[32]

Nobody listened.

On 18 August 1995, it was announced that the leading southern hemisphere players had signed with their unions and would play in officially sanctioned competitions. The World Rugby Corporation dream was over. But the three unions had in effect declared that they were about to go professional.

A little over a week later, on 26 August 1995, IRB chairman Vernon Pugh – that staunch defender of amateur rugby, but, by now, with nowhere to go – announced that rugby would become an open game.

Wales was nowhere near ready for what was to come.

CHAPTER 2

An Open Game

'[It is] a melancholy born of shoulder-hunching
and long-suffering resignation. It is no longer
that of a sudden tragic death.'[1]

(Gerald Davies, quoted in *Rygbi Cymru:
Y Gêm yn y Gwaed*, S4C, 2023)

IN 1995, WALES were awarded the hosting rights for the 1999 Rugby World Cup. Part of the bid included the construction of a brand-new, state-of-the-art national stadium. It had been made clear by the UK government that its Millennium Commission would provide part-funding for a landmark building in Wales. 'A' landmark building. One. There were two major proposals from Wales – a new rugby stadium and a new Zaha Hadid-designed opera house in Cardiff Bay.

On 26 August 1995, Gareth Davies was on holiday in Portugal. Having joined Cardiff Athletic Club as its first chief executive a year or so earlier, he knew that the Cardiff Arms Park site would be key to the overall proposal. The Millennium Commission's decision was imminent.

'So, I had a call and it was BBC Wales and I assumed that they wanted to talk to me about what was happening with the new stadium, and I was pretty hopeful that it would get the decision. But instead, it was "the game has gone open overnight". And I thought, it's August 26th, the season is starting in a fortnight... it was idiocy.'[2]

Huw Jones, then a senior officer and later chief executive with the Sports Council for Wales, thought that the game was unprepared: 'I think it came as a big surprise to a lot of people that it happened, and I don't think they knew how to react. I think all they saw was "well, we can pay people now" and it was nothing much more than that. No review, no strategy behind it. There was no consideration of "well, hang on a minute, what are the implications of this, what are the implications for the game in its totality, what are the implications of this for the clubs? And, therefore, what are the implications for how we actually run clubs and how we make sure that people don't go bust? That the game is actually run properly?" And I don't think there were ever any discussions about that – nothing really changed. And I think, arguably, that attitude and mentality progressed even into recent years. It's gone on for 20 years, that type of mentality. It's just "we'll keep on doing the same old things".'[3]

The situation soon descended into chaos. Jason Smith, who became a players' agent, recalled, 'Professionalism created a culture where everyone was expecting to get paid, however high up or low down the playing ladder you were. In that sense, the situation was unworkable right from the start... About five times every week, as I did the rounds negotiating contracts for my players, I used to think "They're going to go bust". There were no proper business models in place as a rule.'[4]

At Cardiff, a salary structure was hastily assembled.

'I think for the more traditional clubs in Wales and England it was "Bloody hell, how do we manage this transition without any money?"' recalls Gareth Davies. 'One of the issues we had [at Cardiff] was that most of our players were in the Wales squad. So, we had to structure something. We made it that if you were an international player, you got £6,000 a year. If you were a mid-range player [a first-team regular but not an international], you'd get £4,000.

If you were up-and-coming, you'd get £2,000. So that was the budget. Peter [Thomas, Cardiff chairman] put a little bit of money in and then money started coming in, because you could earn money from competitions. The idea was that it would be semi-pro, to start, but becoming more pro, gradually.'[5]

Initially, the excited chatter was all about the players who could now be brought home. Scott Quinnell had become the 164th Wales union international to sign for rugby league in 1994. Now, it was assumed, players wouldn't need to leave for the north of England. Welsh clubs decided that they would raise their profile and bring in supporters in greater numbers by recruiting some star players. Jonathan Davies became one of the first, signing for Cardiff in early 1996.

New competitions were inaugurated – a midweek Anglo-Welsh tournament (in which, alarmingly, weakened English teams routinely thumped their Welsh counterparts) and – minus English and Scottish representation for its first season – a new European tournament.

Performances in Europe were respectable. Pontypridd beat Milan in their first game, but then narrowly lost to Leinster. Swansea lost to Munster but beat Castres to progress to the semi-finals. Cardiff drew away to Bordeaux Bègles, thrashed Ulster and then in the semi-finals dispatched Leinster with relative ease at a sparsely populated Lansdowne Road on the penultimate day of 1995. Swansea were thumped in Toulouse by the home team on the same day, who squeaked to the inaugural European Cup by beating Cardiff in extra time at the National Stadium.

But very quickly the balance of economic power in these islands became apparent. For every exiled player brought back from rugby league, two or three would leave. Not, this time, for the rival code, but for rugby union clubs. Former Wales captain Gareth Llewellyn went to Harlequins, his brother Glyn to Wasps. Colin Stephens and Phil Davies left

Llanelli for Leeds. The Cardiff half-backs Andy Moore and Adrian Davies went as a pair to Richmond on a reported £65,000 a year where, over the next year or so, they would be joined by Barry Williams, John Davies and Craig Quinnell. Just as alarmingly, players who were tempted back from rugby league often chose English union clubs – Scott Quinnell joined his brother at Richmond, while Allan Bateman also signed up. It was perhaps unsurprising that English clubs were able to build such impressive squads. Ashley Levett, for instance, pumped £8m into Richmond, allowing the club to run monthly wage bills – and this is just for the players – of around £230,000.[6] At Gosforth, John Hall bought the club, relocated it to Newcastle, renamed it the Falcons and brought All Black and rugby league great Va'aiga Tuigamala in for £1m.

In an unusual approach to the kind of sequencing one might expect, the WRU made three key appointments in reverse order of seniority. First, they appointed Dave Clark from South Africa to lead on player conditioning. Then they appointed Kevin Bowring as coach to the men's national team. Finally, Terry Cobner was appointed its first full-time director of rugby to work above the national team coach.

In 1996 Bowring's Wales performed creditably in pushing England all the way at Twickenham, came within a missed conversion kick of a draw with Scotland, before beating France in the final game of the season. That summer's tour of Australia went badly. Wales could create and score plenty, but they conceded more.

Looking around the new landscape in the southern hemisphere, Cobner saw that all three of the major nations had streamlined their top tiers. Australia had decided on three fully professional teams, South Africa on four, broadly based on their existing state or provincial structures. New Zealand had settled on five, based on five existing provinces but with extended areas to bring in provinces excluded from the new structure. They would play in a new, half-season-long Super 12 competition, with the traditional provinces continuing in their domestic competitions.

Cobner saw merit in a new tier above the existing twelve-team Welsh Division 1. He believed there to be around 45 to 50 players in Wales who could make it as professionals, with maybe 15 or so coming up through the age grades. His vision was for no more than four professional teams.

He was too late. About 18 months too late. A tug of war – between the WRU and the clubs in which first one, then the other, offered contracts to the leading players – had been won by the clubs. They now held the registrations of the leading players and they would decide who those players would represent.

The feeding frenzy was in full swing. With bank accounts boosted by transfer fees paid by English clubs to prize away Welsh assets, Welsh clubs in turn started to splash out, most notoriously Llanelli in signing the great All Black and rugby league fly-half Frano Botica. His signing – for a reputed transfer fee of £85,000 – became a byword for the profligacy of Welsh club rugby in the late 1990s. It is an unfair reputation.

Ron Jones, brought on to the Llanelli board in 1997 to try to mend some of the errors of the initial years of professionalism, takes up the story: 'There's no question that the club had been misled by a local businessman and it had spent his money before the money had come in. That was what really caused the trouble... this businessman had more or less promised that he would cover Frano's costs. And he didn't put a penny in. He was great friends with Phil Bennett, which gave his money credibility, but the reality was that there was nothing there.'[7]

By 1997 several clubs were in serious trouble, with widespread reports that the WRU had made loans totalling over £1m to five top-flight clubs.[8] Llanelli and Swansea had the largest single loans, with Bridgend, Newbridge and Treorchy of the first division clubs and Aberavon and Abertillery in the second tier also needing support. Even so, clubs started cancelling player contracts, with the likes of rugby league returnees Kevin Ellis and Rowland Phillips offloaded mid-season by Treorchy. Meanwhile, out west, Llanelli found themselves as much as £900,000 in debt and having to sell their Stradey Park home to the WRU and then lease it back.

Cobner's wish to reduce the number of clubs at the top level was partially realised that summer. Mid-season, it was decided that the traditional two-down, two-up system of promotion and relegation would be replaced with a four-down, none-up alternative. Caerphilly, Treorchy and Newbridge were adrift and doomed to relegation. The last of the four to drop came down to final-day tussle between Newport, Neath – astonishingly, just a year after winning the title – and Dunvant. The Swansea club were the fall-guys. Aberavon and Llandovery – who finished first and second in Division 2 – were denied promotion.

The 1997–98 season was catastrophic. The national team's predilection for scoring a lot but conceding many more continued at Twickenham, where an unprecedented four-try, 26-point haul mattered little as England ran in eight tries for an equally unfathomable 60 points. Gritty victories over Scotland and Ireland followed, before the knack of conceding a shed-full reappeared at Wembley against France – this time without the consolation of creating much themselves – in yet another record defeat by 51–0.

In his end of championship report, Bowring made a number of far-reaching recommendations. He wanted to see a distinctive Welsh way of playing developed and four regions to be formed to compete in a new Celtic League. He also wanted to see a wider implementation of the existing, but extremely limited, central contracts system for leading players. Derwyn Jones had arguably become the first player in the world to openly make his living entirely from rugby, in June 1995 – before the game had actually gone pro – when he resigned from the police force to work full-time for the WRU as a development officer (with regular appearances for the national team part of his role). A package deal with the WRU agreed in 1996 boosted his earnings – taking payments for his WRU job alongside playing for Cardiff and Wales into account – to around £70,000 a year.[9] Bowring's report was largely ignored – at least in the short term – and he left his post.

The season had descended into a series of disputes between the WRU and its leading clubs.

With senior clubs in dire financial straits, the WRU presented all eight premier division clubs with a ten-year loyalty agreement, in which the clubs would undertake to play only in WRU-sanctioned competitions for the next decade.

Refusal meant no payment of competition and television monies by the WRU to the clubs. Cardiff, Swansea and Newport started to think about a future beyond the reach of the WRU. By the spring, the leading clubs were considering strike action.

The construction of the new Millennium Stadium had severely impacted upon Cardiff's ability to generate income at their stadium next door. At one stage, there was a proposal – supported by the local authority – to build a brand-new stadium for Cardiff RFC in Cardiff Bay. Between the objections of some members of the Athletic Club and a cooling on the part of the authority, the final plan reverted to a redevelopment of the current site, with Cardiff RFC remaining where they were.

The nature of the proposed redevelopment meant that at least part of the structure would 'oversail' Cardiff Athletic Club property. Cardiff took legal advice which suggested that they would be entitled to a significant, multi-million-pound compensation payment for allowing the new stadium to overhang their land.

'We weren't stupid,' said Gareth Davies later. 'We would never have held them [the WRU] to ransom for millions. We would have been national pariahs.'

Cardiff offered to allow work to continue for a figure which was in the region of six, rather than eight, figures. Vernon Pugh, in his role as WRU chairman, refused to accept Cardiff's offer. Suspicion grew that the separate issues of the construction of the stadium and the loyalty agreement which Cardiff were refusing to sign were becoming conflated.

'I think Vernon Pugh basically said, "we aren't going to do a deal with them on the property, because that will tide them over and allow them not to sign the agreement".'

Shortly after the referendum in 1997 which established devolution in Wales, the Secretary of State, Ron Davies, collared Gareth Davies at a dinner.

'He came up to me and said, "Can you tell me what all this mess is about at the stadium?", because they were about £3m to £4m short of being able to finish the walkway along the river. They had no money left to do that and they couldn't open the stadium without it, they needed it for access and egress. So, he came up to me saying, "Look, we need to sort this and you need to tell me the truth." I met him and his officials on the Monday and they basically had the whole truth and nothing but the truth. They were extremely nervous about giving money to the union, so they wanted to know exactly what had been going on. I don't know how much of a part that played, but after that meeting and after they'd done their due diligence, the union got the money and the stadium went ahead. That's pretty important to remember when people say that Cardiff spoiled the stadium.'[10]

The impact of the union's decision not to settle with Cardiff cost Laing, the construction company, millions of pounds in adjustments to the stadium. Laing eventually lost at least £26m on the project, laid off 800 employees and withdrew from the construction business.

Amidst the turmoil, the WRU sought to pour oil on troubled waters by firing the national team's coaches and sending the team off for a tour of South Africa, then-world champions and still smarting from defeat to the Lions the previous year. Dennis John and Lynn Howells were given the unenviable task of taking the coaching reins.

If the Five Nations was awful, this was something else entirely. A run of morale-sapping defeats to provincial teams was less than ideal preparation for the one-off Test which – to this point, at least – remains probably the lowest moment in Welsh international rugby history. Only a series of clumsy fumbles by rampant attackers prevented the Springboks from running in a century. They eventually fell just four points short – their 96–13 victory still, by some distance, a record margin between two founder members of the IRB.

After the tour, John and Howells were quickly dispensed with. In a sign of dysfunction within the union, Terry Cobner opened negotiations with Mike Ruddock about taking over, while Glanmor Griffiths and Vernon Pugh were on their way out to Australia, where Graham Henry was waiting for them. And, as Alun Carter suggests in *Seeing Red*, 'Vernon always got what he wanted at that time.'[11]

Yet Ruddock had a serious shot at the role in 1998. Indeed, Ian Gough recalls, in his autobiography, receiving a memo outlining arrangements for the tour: 'I remember that while the planning was going on for the tour, there was a memo sent out clearly stating that, on the first day, Swansea coach Mike Ruddock would be addressing the squad. Now, it must have been pretty close to happening for them to have sent that out – I don't know how close – but three weeks before the tour, the union opted to put Pontypridd coaches Dennis John and Lynn Howells in charge.'[12]

By mid August, the consensus was that the domestic structure had to be strengthened, with fewer games but of far higher quality required to both ensure the clubs were viable businesses and to adequately prepare the best players for the rigours of Test rugby. Llanelli's chairman Ron Jones was convinced that: 'We don't have a game that is viable in terms of structure or playing standards. Unless we confront the issues, then we will go rapidly downhill and the game in Wales will die.'[13]

Even the WRU agreed, having started to discuss the idea, at the very last minute, of a British league which would feature 20 teams – 14 English, four Welsh and two Scottish – in two conferences of ten.

And yet – in a move which became wearily predictable – the WRU's line was broadly that they of course supported the clubs, but the time was not right for a cross-border competition. The time would never be right. Cardiff chief executive Gareth Davies felt that 'every hurdle has been put in our way which makes you think it is some kind of smokescreen and there is a deeper agenda.'[14]

Neath succumbed to financial pressures – with debts of £645,000 and 13 players leaving – and went to the wall. They were re-established under new parent company Gower Park Ltd, owned by the WRU.

'It didn't say anything,' says Gareth Davies now of the loyalty agreement. 'We didn't know what we were signing up to. It was a horrible time. We ended up in the High Court in London. It was "Look, sign up now, for ten years, with people who've got no commercial experience at all"... We had pretty serious people on the board who knew what they were talking about. If it had been a two-year deal, to get us over this hump, until the game restructures... but then you couldn't really see how the game was going to restructure.'[15]

Matters came to a head on 20 August as Cardiff and Swansea confirmed that the WRU would not allow them to compete in the premier division. 'We never said we wouldn't play,' Davies argued, 'only that we wouldn't sign the ten-year deal. For that we've been kicked out.'[16] They therefore arranged a season of friendly matches with the 14 Allied Dunbar Premiership One clubs. The matches were not sanctioned by either union, so junior or retired referees were brought in to officiate. BBC Wales – who had recently lost the rights to the Welsh premier division – won the broadcast rights for the matches.

By 24 August, five days before the first game of the season, the WRU confirmed the expulsion of the two clubs – although they would still be permitted to compete in the Challenge Cup, at least partly due to pressure from sponsors. Newport – who had been relegated from the premier division the previous season, were suddenly reinstated, while Aberavon were promoted, alongside champions Caerphilly.

The new season began with an away win for Cardiff at Bedford before a thumping victory over Saracens at the Arms Park. The 10,000-strong crowd compared favourably with an aggregate attendance of only 8,200 at the four Welsh premier division matches played that same weekend.[17] Further west, Swansea started with a home victory over West Hartlepool before beating Wasps away. The pattern continued for the next few months, with the two rebel clubs regularly playing in front of large home crowds, Cardiff averaging 10,000-strong crowds in the first half of the season compared to 4,000 the previous year, and the Cardiff v Swansea derby in January 1999 played in front of 14,000.

The clubs which had stayed behind struggled – both to attract crowds and to produce quality rugby.

The European season, for those who had stayed, was torrid. On the first weekend of the Heineken Cup, Pontypridd were the only Welsh winners, in Glasgow. Llanelli lost at home to Leinster in front of 2,000 people, Neath shipped 50 points at home to Perpignan in front of a handful more, while Ebbw Vale were demolished by 108–16 in Toulouse (they eventually conceded 307 points in six games, somehow managing to gain revenge over Toulouse in the reverse fixture). Llanelli and Pontypridd limped into the quarter-finals, where both were comfortably dispatched by French opposition.

The WRU resurrected the idea of a British league for the

1999–2000 season, with Terry Cobner said to be suggesting that four Welsh super clubs – Llanelli, Swansea, Cardiff and either Newport or Pontypridd – should feature.[18] By the end of the year, plans appeared to be advancing, with the Irish Rugby Football Union now thought to be interested and Pontypridd now favoured to be the fourth Welsh super club in a four-nation, two-conference, 24-club competition.

The reaction was lukewarm. Of the two proposed conferences, the one containing ten English and two Welsh clubs was the one everybody wanted to be in and not the other which included four Welsh clubs, four Irish provinces and two Scottish super clubs.

As 1999 dawned, the IRFU had withdrawn from discussions and the Scottish Rugby Union feared that they were being pushed out of an Anglo-Welsh League. They were right. By mid January, the proposal was for a 20-club Anglo-Welsh tournament, again in two conferences, this time with seven English and three Welsh clubs in each.

Later that month, Cardiff and Swansea were invited to a meeting with the full WRU general committee. Anticipating an attempt on the union's behalf at some sort of rapprochement, the Cardiff delegation attempted to run a presentation from a laptop. It brought an admonishment from the committee as they had not been granted permission to bring any devices into the meeting, their presentation was met with blank faces and silence and it degenerated from there, with the general committee demanding to know the value of the television deal negotiated by the rebel clubs, only to be told to mind their own business.

Under IRB pressure over the continued unsanctioned rebel matches, the WRU fined Cardiff and Swansea £150,000 each – £60,000 for playing the matches, the same amount for negotiating their own independent television deals, and a further £30,000 for allowing their matches to be refereed by unapproved officials. The RFU were effectively sanctioned by the International Rugby Board (IRB) – by withholding IRB trust grants worth £60,000 – for not doing enough to prevent the rebel matches. The fractious nature of the relationship between the English clubs and the RFU had reached the European Commission, where English First Division Rugby (EFDR) had lodged a complaint against the RFU for restraint of trade, seeking control of the competitions in which they played.

On 31 January 1999, the key players met in Tewkesbury to discuss the proposed Anglo-Welsh League. Swansea and Cardiff now had seats on English First Division Rugby and were effectively part of the English delegation. The two clubs were asked by the RFU to suggest a figure for how many clubs the WRU would accept in an Anglo-Welsh League. There were rumblings about the future of some senior English clubs, including West Hartlepool, Richmond, London Scottish and Bedford. If those clubs were to fold, there might be space for a similar number of Welsh clubs.

Glanmor Griffiths and Terry Cobner walked in together and were asked for their thoughts on the number of Welsh clubs which should be put forward for the new tournament. They wanted ten. They were offered five – two in the top division and three in the second. Griffiths and Cobner immediately left the room for a private discussion. When they returned, Griffiths flatly rejected the offer and left, criticising it as 'demeaning', while Cobner was angered by the English clubs' assumption that they would decide which Welsh clubs would play in which division.

The English delegation was almost as amazed at the WRU's response as were the representatives from Cardiff and Swansea. The RFU's then-chairman Brian Baister said: 'I think the Anglo-Welsh League would have been successful. Every member of the Wales national squad would have been a part of it and I had no doubt that within a year Wales would have had four clubs in the top division. It is clear the supporters in England and Wales are in favour of a cross-border tournament and we tried desperately hard to bring it about.'[19]

'If you look at it from today's perspective, with Glanmor saying that we needed our top ten or twelve clubs in the new system – that was never going to work,' said Llanelli's Ron Jones many years later. 'If you look at the nature of professionalism, the nature of the money that was in the game... say there were 20 clubs in the Anglo-Welsh League, common sense tells you that we couldn't put up more than two or three, maybe four clubs who could be competitive at that level. So, we'd have reached the same point we're at today. All that work, and the future which was rejected in order to protect those clubs, has led to those clubs disappearing anyway because they weren't sustainable in a professional age. Now, if we had succeeded in getting five in, perhaps the same would have happened as is now happening in England – they wouldn't all have succeeded. We see three that have gone now [Wasps, Worcester and London Irish all went into administration and dropped out of the top tier of English rugby in 2022–23]. The economic effect might have led to the same point that we're at today, but we'd have done so from a position of greater strength.'[20]

The arrival of Graham Henry as the new national coach the previous autumn had immediately improved performances – the 83-point margin of the Pretoria defeat in June was reduced to just eight against the same opponents by November, with Wales level late in the game. Ahead of his first Five Nations championship, Henry had supported a reduction in the number of elite teams and backed the WRU's decision to 'reject this paltry offer. The whole idea was to improve rugby in Wales, Scotland and England after Ireland decided not to take part... What was proposed wasn't British, just a few Welsh clubs in a predominantly English league which would have been no good to anyone.'[21]

'It was a disastrous decision, without question,' countered

Gareth Davies. 'It was a huge opportunity lost. An Anglo-Welsh would have enabled us to be strong and build the business. When you are playing against the likes of Bath, Exeter, Gloucester and Bristol – four teams just 60, 70 miles away – you're looking at putting 2,000 on the gate each week with travelling fans. The business model starts to work then.'

The journalist Peter Jackson agreed: 'At that time, there was no question the major Welsh clubs would have enhanced the quality of the English Premiership. The mistake the WRU made was thinking England needed as many as eight or even ten Welsh clubs.'[22]

The national team's fortunes revived with joyous wins over France in Paris, England at Wembley, a successful two-Test tour of Argentina and, later that summer, revenge for the South African humiliation a year earlier with a first-ever win over the Springboks in Cardiff. But, beneath Test level, the game was in pieces.

The rebels' race was run. English clubs increasingly fielded reserve teams as the season wore on. Matches which had attracted 10,000-plus crowds were now attracting as few as 2,000 and, even then, with tickets reduced to £5.[23] Swansea raged against the dying of the light, thumping Llanelli in the SWALEC Cup final at Ninian Park. Scott Gibbs' post-match comments have become as infamous as they are inaccurately recalled. 'To be honest, from what I've seen, Llanelli have been playing against boys. This time they were up against men and they were out-muscled, out-played and out-manoeuvred.'[24]

The rebels agreed to return to the Welsh fold in June. In return for places in the WRU premier division and Heineken Cup, they both signed eight-year loyalty agreements with the WRU and agreed to play only in WRU-sanctioned competitions in the 1999–2000 season. They secured the WRU's agreement that they would be allowed to join an Anglo-Welsh tournament, if one could be agreed, for the beginning of the 2000–01 season.

That tournament never came.

CHAPTER 3

Ruck the WRU

'It seems to me the future of Welsh rugby
was decided by a bloke and his twelve-hour night shift.'[1]

(Mike Hill, Llantwit Major RFC)

WALES' TEN-MATCH WINNING run after that thrilling victory
in Paris in March 1999 came to an end in an echo of 1991 – in
Cardiff, in a Rugby World Cup pool match, against Samoa.
They progressed through the pool stages this time despite
that defeat but were again deposited from the tournament
in familiar fashion – by an Australian team which went on to
win the trophy.

It had not been a good tournament for any of the nations
of these islands. Wales were the only one of the four to make
it through as pool winners. The other three had to negotiate
a never-repeated repechage round in which the five pool
runners-up, plus the best third-placed team, faced off for one
of three places in the quarter-finals proper. Ireland exited
to Argentina, Scotland beat Samoa for the dubious honour
of facing New Zealand, while England also made it through
before an apparently endless stream of drop goals by South
Africa's Jannie de Beer dumped them out of the competition.
It was the first time that none of the four had reached the
semi-finals.

Alan Hosie, chair of the Five Nations committee, urged
the unions to look afresh at the structure of elite rugby in the

northern hemisphere. Convening a meeting of the unions on 15 November, he urged greater co-operation, including fresh consideration of a cross-border league.

The WRU had already agreed with the SRU that the 1999–2000 season would be the first of a new – and, it was assumed, temporary – Welsh-Scottish premiership as a prelude to a full-blown British (and possibly Irish) league the following year.

Yet, as Smith and Williams saw, 'At the domestic level, Welsh rugby in 1999 is still a war zone of unexploded mines, mud-filled craters, empty shells and the terminally wounded fighting for life while the general staff close ranks and look to salvation from the retro-roofed phoenix rising from the debris alongside the Taff.'

The domestic game had to change, they thought: 'This is, principally, the chronic disunity in the game, a product of a sport's structure which once fitted and no longer does the social reality of a particular society and its aspirations. The social integument of Wales has changed. Its new institutions must reflect that deep change and in rugby terms too, aspirations, to be successful, will inevitably be subsumed by the larger reality and image of Wales. Graham Henry sees both the regional dream of Ray Williams and the traditions of great Welsh clubs secured in the concept of four or five "super" clubs. It is, for sure, a way forward for Welsh rugby to claim once more a rightful place on the fields of praise, but only if Wales itself really means more than anything else. The alternative, for sure, is retreat from those fields forever.'[2]

A new financial agreement had been reached between the WRU and the clubs which rewarded on-field success in domestic and European competition. Leading players were signed up on what were effectively dual contracts – partly paid by their clubs, partly by the WRU. The effect was that the top five or six clubs were becoming ever stronger and the gap between them and the already-struggling became vast. Cardiff's 106–0 win over Dunvant prompted Cardiff benefactor Peter Thomas to express concern about the safety of semi-professionals facing bigger, stronger, fully professional opponents.[3]

The concentration of resources appeared to have some impact in Europe. Llanelli and Cardiff faced each other in the Heineken Cup quarter-final – the first and still only occasion on which two Welsh teams have played each other in the last eight of the continent's premier tournament. Llanelli won but were eliminated at the semi-final stage by a last-minute Northampton penalty in Reading. Such heartbreak would become a familiar feeling for the Scarlets in Europe.

Nevertheless, it had been quite an experience for Llanelli, as Ron Jones recalls: 'Reading then held around 25,000. Northampton brought 5,000 supporters from just up the road. We took up 15,000. What was interesting was that – I came up with this idea – you buy a busload of tickets and we'll provide the bus... we had 130 buses going up from Wales to watch the Scarlets – only a quarter of them came from the Llanelli area. There was something about the brand, something about how they felt the Scarlets was part of them, that had succeeded in lighting a flame. And I don't forget that.'[4]

Elsewhere, Newport began to wake from a long slumber as a new investor, Tony Brown, arrived to fund the signing of world-renowned stars such as Gary Teichmann and Adrian Garvey, along with Welsh stars Shane Howarth, Peter Rogers, and David Llewellyn. The perception that Wales had only so many quality players to go around was strengthened by the transfer merry-go-round – while Newport and others were recruiting, Pontypridd were losing Ian Gough, Geraint Lewis, Neil Jenkins and Martyn Williams.

'It wasn't just the rugby, it was also what they were doing off the pitch [at Newport] that attracted me, the innovative community and commercial stuff,' wrote Ian Gough. 'In Wales they were truly ahead of the game, doing things that no other club were and that was reflected in the way crowds had exploded at Rodney Parade.'[5]

At international level, the optimism of the previous season quickly dissipated. After the memorable victories of 1999 in Paris and at Wembley, France exacted their revenge with a 36–3 win in Cardiff, while England's was even more brutal – a 46–12 defeat forcing widespread changes to the team which had performed so creditably the previous year.

Worse was to come. Conditioning coach and squad father figure Steve Black felt the criticism of the physical readiness of the players so keenly that he resigned mid-season. Two of the key players of that run – the New Zealanders Shane Howarth and Brett Sinkinson – had assured the WRU that they qualified for Wales through their grandparents. Nobody thought to check. A Sunday newspaper article published midway through the Six Nations suggested that neither were eligible. Both were immediately stood down from the national squad.

'Brett had no idea he was Welsh until Graham phoned up and told him that he was,'[6] said Byron Hayward, rather uncharitably.

A wildly erratic 2001 Six Nations – a record home defeat to England, a second consecutive victory in Paris for the first time since 1957, a record home defeat to Ireland in the foot-and-mouth delayed conclusion to the tournament in October – led to further unrest.

The costs of running the professional game were becoming unsustainable. Peter Thomas at Cardiff pointed out that benefactors had ploughed enormous sums – the precise figure is unclear but estimates at the time varied between £15m and £20m – into the professional game in a little over five years. Gareth Jenkins at Llanelli warned that clubs were spending over their budgets on player salaries in an attempt to both remain within the elite tier and to be competitive in Europe. Tony Brown, at Newport, concurred, arguing that: 'Players are getting too much money. It has gone beyond anything since I came in a few years ago. Players in Wales are the most highly paid in Europe, which is not on, given our resources.'

Departing Wales team manager David Pickering agreed and suggested a solution: 'There are too many mediocre players. The answer is to make the professional product and the professional player more elite by having fewer.'[7]

After another season of relative failure in Europe (Cardiff and Swansea had reached the quarter-finals of the Heineken Cup but were comfortably beaten), those who saw themselves as the pre-eminent clubs in Wales – Bridgend, Cardiff, Llanelli, Newport and Swansea – took up Pickering's challenge and launched Rugby Partnership Wales (RPW) Ltd in May 2001. By October, the Gang of Five had become the Gang of Six as Pontypridd joined them.

Their aims were revolutionary. The top-flight should be reduced to six clubs. A joint venture should be created between the six clubs and the WRU to manage the elite game, led by a professional executive charged with increasing revenue. A national academy system should be jointly established by clubs and the union. And a fund should be instituted to improve facilities at the leading clubs.[8]

Ideas for new structures fizzed around the rugby firmament. Clive Rowlands favoured an eight-team top-flight from August to December, then four provinces for European rugby between January and March, with the Six Nations following in the spring. John Dawes saw no need for regions at all, arguing: 'I'd simply say that if you look back to the old days, when we had four quality teams – Cardiff, Swansea, Llanelli, Newport – we seemed able to compete with the best.'[9]

It was understood at the time that Wales coach Graham Henry favoured three or four elite teams. Some said he favoured three regions. An interview with Henry, carried in a Cardiff RFC match programme in January 1999, quoted him saying that he believed there to be enough quality Welsh-qualified players to populate four elite teams in a British or Anglo-Welsh League (with perhaps one or two top-class overseas players).[10] However, it later emerged that he felt that there were, in fact, enough players of quality in Wales to sustain only two regions with playing squads of around 35. His favoured option would have been east and west Wales, or if pushed possibly Gwent, Glamorgan and Carmarthenshire, but he recognised that 'village-ism' would get in the way.[11]

Also standing in the way of all of these ideas – whether four provinces or five or six clubs – was the 1998 loyalty agreement demanded of the clubs by the WRU, which had guaranteed an eight-team top-flight in Wales for ten years. Now that Swansea and Cardiff were back in the fold, there were eight signatories. Getting out of that agreement would be challenging and costly.

While the Welsh-Scottish season staggered on to little interest – one Friday night game between Swansea and Pontypridd attracted an official crowd of just 932 – the stakes were raised. The Gang of Six developed proposals contained within a document, presented to the WRU, titled 'Partnership and Professionalism for a Vibrant and Viable Game'.[12] At the launch, Stuart Gallacher of Llanelli insisted that the proposals needed to be implemented if Welsh rugby was to avoid bankruptcy. Clubs required £3m a year to flourish in the new landscape, but at best were surviving on half that, with benefactors expected to make up the difference. Six clubs, funded through a mixture of WRU payments, benefactor investment and commercial income, could work. Four centrally-owned and run regions could not.[13] If benefactors had poured in £15m to £20m in five years or so of professional rugby, the WRU had saved itself that £15m to £20m (although that figure could be much higher, with Leighton Samuel claiming to have put £4.5m into Bridgend in just three years).[14] And without benefactor money, regions were a non-starter.

On the field, the decline continued. In the new Celtic League tournament, Welsh teams won just two of 21 matches against Irish opposition. All four Irish provinces reached the quarter-finals, while the three Welsh teams who made it through all lost in Ireland at that stage. An all-Ireland final was won by Leinster. In Europe, Llanelli were the only team to make it through the Heineken Cup pool stages, where they again suffered semi-final heartbreak against English opposition – this time a last-minute Leicester penalty which contrived to hit both post and crossbar before trickling over.

In the 2002 Six Nations, Wales seemed to have wound back the clock to the early 1990s. A record 54–10 defeat to Ireland – who became the sixth Test team to rack up a half-century against Wales since 1988 – led to Graham Henry's resignation. In echoes of the previous decade, there were insinuations that general committee members had undermined the national coach. Gareth Edwards, for one, was furious, criticising the comments of WRU general committee vice-chairman Les Williams who had called on Henry to resign: 'I thought his outburst was scandalous and the fact they haven't taken him to task conjures up all kinds of thoughts like whether it was a set-up in the first place.'[15]

Unlike those earlier departures, fewer people were now willing to accept that the head coach was solely responsible. The English coach Dick Best had prophesied the previous week that: 'The WRU need to make some brutal decisions and quickly because they are on a slippery slope and the easiest way off it would be to sack Henry. Yet that would not make the serious faults in their structure disappear. Yet scapegoats and sport seem synonymous these days and the Welsh have never been shy in that department. The union have not had the courage to implement Henry's system, which would take time to bear fruit and, like the Irish structure, create the right environment. My money's on the Welsh taking the easy way out!'[16]

Ieuan Evans agreed: 'Getting rid of the coach is not going

to be the panacea to all our ills. If people think that is going to happen then they are very much mistaken. But the problems within Welsh rugby run far deeper than anything to do with the coach.'

Evans' thoughts were echoed by former Wales captain Gwyn Jones, who saw an opportunity to significantly improve the structure of Welsh rugby, 'What I hope this will highlight is that it is not possible for one man to change the foundations of Welsh rugby. There needs to be a radical overhaul of the game in Wales, there is no other option.'[17]

Alun Carter and Nick Bishop, part of the analysis team for several Welsh coaches throughout the 1990s and 2000s, saw an issue which may echo into the present day: 'the balance between having a successful coach and a successful support structure beneath him clearly wasn't right. When Graham inevitably started to lose a few games, there was nothing and no one for him to fall back on.'[18]

As Frank Keating wrote a few days later, 'the grim-faced man may have gone but the grim structure remains.'[19]

It was a sign of the depths to which Wales had sunk that a 50–10 defeat to England at Twickenham drew a collective sigh of relief. It hadn't been as bad as many had feared. And the match almost didn't happen at all, with talk that Rugby Partnership Wales might withhold their players from the match unless the WRU reopened talks. Having secured the WRU's agreement that they would reduce the top-flight to six clubs as soon as it was legally practicable, and with rumours circulating that the six had secured agreement to payments of up to £1.5m per club within the new structure – the match went ahead.

Having given the Gang of Six the impression of support, the WRU general committee decided to put the proposal to all member clubs at a special general meeting. It was widely thought that they had done so in the certain knowledge that it would fail.

Marcus Russell, Ebbw Vale's chairman, agreed. The WRU's commitment to making the change when legally practicable meant – given the existence of the loyalty agreements signed in the late 1990s – that no change could be made for at least another five years.

'We have been conned by the WRU who promised us change only to pass the buck to the whole membership, which means that amateurs will be voting on the future of the professional game,' said Bridgend owner Leighton Samuel. 'The union's instinct for self-preservation is so sharp that it has removed the two bullets we had in our revolver (the possibility of strike action by the players ahead of the Scotland and England Six Nations games) without having conceded anything.'[20]

The WRU – having spent 20 years in reactive mode – eventually tried to take a lead. For over a year, a working party it had commissioned, under the leadership of its president Sir Tasker Watkins, had been developing ideas for the future structure and administration of the game. The working party was tasked with conducting 'a comprehensive review of the structures of and ways in which Welsh rugby is governed and to propose appropriate recommendations for change.' Sir Tasker added, 'Our aim is to provide a blueprint of an organisation fit to meet the demands of the professional game and serve a return to amateurism to the extent that that is appropriate.'[21]

The membership of the working party had been drawn from the WRU general committee, WRU staff and independent members consisting of three respected former internationals in Gerald Davies, Ken Jones and Gwyn Jones.

Ray Williams welcomed the inclusion of independent members, noting that this addition gave the working party a chance. The union's decision-making process was 'convoluted, cumbersome, slow and completely out of kilter with the requirements of a high-profile governing body'.[22] His warning – that while it would be the clubs who would make the decision, they would to a large extent be guided by the WRU general committee – proved depressingly prescient.

During its lifespan, five general committee members who had sat on the working party – David Pickering, Mike Farley, Glanmor Griffiths, Howard Watkins and David Rees – withdrew their support.

By late 2001, Gerald Davies – one of the independent members of the Sir Tasker Watkins group – was writing that the WRU general committee had received a draft of the working party's report and had decided that they would reject almost all of the recommendations it contained. The working party was not even afforded the courtesy of the opportunity to present their findings to the general committee. Griffiths had instead started to develop his own counter-proposals.

'The turkeys have voted against Christmas,' said Stephen Jones in the *Sunday Times*, arguing that Griffiths' proposals amounted to nothing more than 'cosmetic shuffling'.[23]

Amidst all of this, supporters were not taken particularly seriously by the WRU. The money which supporters brought in was welcome, but not essential, in the amateur era. But now the WRU had to contend with something they had never previously had to face – collective action by disgruntled fans.

During the late 1990s the widespread emergence of the internet allowed – in the words of Glanmor Griffiths – 'any Tom, Dick or Harry' to express an opinion on the running of the game.[24]

Gwladrugby.com, set up by a group of young Welsh supporters making their way in London and missing the comforts of home, was among the first. Dan Allsobrook, one its original editors, takes up the story:

'We played up to that epithet and took pleasure in taking the piss out of Glanmor's grandiose management style. The WRU commissioned a working party, led by WRU president Sir Tasker Watkins QC VC. It was a massive piece of work and the working party consisted of some of the biggest names in Welsh rugby at the time and, crucially, a number of WRU board members including Glanmor himself. There was more than a sniff of marking your own homework from the get-go.

'When it became clear that the working party's findings and recommendations weren't going to be to Glanmor's liking, he resigned from the working party and embarked on a parallel initiative of his own. He promptly set about undermining the working party and went on a PR tour of the community clubs, armed with a glossy brochure which might as well have had "STATUS QUO" written at the top in big letters.

'As was the case with anything controversial relating to the WRU back then, this stitch-up was conveniently ignored by Glanmor's friends at the *Western Mail* and BBC Wales. Luckily for us, some of the more balanced and worldly journalists down in London wrote some pretty damning copy about how Welsh rugby was about to destroy itself, again. I'm not sure how much that cut through with the rugby-mad Welsh public, but us Gwladers got very hot under the collar about it.

'We also decided that something needed to be done. Although the WRU never published the working party report, we had got hold of a copy. There were a few decent people on the inside with access to information who wanted to help us. We wrote a barrage of articles, trying to explain why governance reform was necessary and how a professional tier needed to be formed without fear or favour. We pleaded with the WRU member clubs to vote for Sir Tasker's reforms. We raised a petition, which garnered over 6,000 signatures. We organised a protest outside WRU HQ on the day of our home Six Nations match against Scotland in April 2002. About 100 of us were there to see our esteemed colleague Terry hand over the petition to WRU secretary Dennis Gethin, who probably just chucked it straight in the bin. But through a lot of hard work, we had managed to attract a lot of media attention that day. I'm not sure what lasting effect it had, but at least we had tried and people had finally taken notice.'[25]

A poll in the *Welsh Mirror* found that 97% of respondents wanted to see the general committee scrapped as 'most fans believe the committee, led by chairman Glanmor Griffiths, is destroying Welsh rugby'.[26]

The reaction was equally furious in the offline world.

Outgoing WRU vice-chairman Les Williams accused the governing body of a lack of leadership: 'It's about time the clubs saw this and did something about it. Unless they have a professional body running the professional game – and the rest of the game run by a Welsh Rugby Union council or whatever it may be – Welsh rugby will go down the same road as Welsh soccer.'[27]

Richard Williams, in the *Guardian*, reflecting on the struggles of recent rugby league convert Iestyn Harris as he settled into the union code, saw hope for Harris, if not for Wales: 'If he can one day destroy an England defence as efficiently as his own administrators have destroyed the morale of Welsh rugby, the investment will have been worthwhile.'[28]

In the first of 2002's special or emergency general meetings of the full membership of the WRU, the Gang of Six had their proposal to reduce the top-flight to six professional teams thrown out by the membership by 325 votes to 98. The Six – knowing full well where a vote of the membership would lead – sat in silence while the general committee made their presentation. None spoke in support. Delegates who spoke from the floor were extremely critical of the general committee, with many referencing the need to fully consider the Tasker Watkins working party's forthcoming report. Rushing into a restructure of one element of the game without addressing governance could not stand.

No sooner had April's SGM finished than another was called, this time for 24 May to discuss the working party's recommendations. The general committee also insisted on filling the agenda with its own counter-proposals.

The great and the good came out to support the working

party. Cliff Morgan prayed that the recommendations would be implemented in full. Ray Williams posited that anything less than the full implementation of the report would be a failure. The country's First Minister, Rhodri Morgan, said that the WRU were drinking in the last chance saloon.[29]

The meeting heard stirring contributions from Gerald Davies and other members of the working party, pushing the case for change. The overall vote on the report was carried, just, by 207 votes to 204. It wasn't enough, as the WRU's constitution required the support of 75% of delegates for such significant changes. The meeting then went through each of the working party's recommendations – none were carried with the required majority.

The *Western Mail*'s report on the meeting made for dispiriting reading: 'when they heard Glanmor Griffiths tell them they would "lose control of the union to outsiders", they promptly allowed themselves to be led by the nose by Mr Griffiths and his self-preservation society on the general committee. And what of the men who were charged with making these decisions? Some were so confused that they put their crosses on the wrong ballot papers after a clear instruction from the chair about which resolution was being voted on. Thirty-one made this mistake on one vote and would have rendered the vote invalid had it been close. At one point a voice rang out, "What exactly are we voting for?"'[30]

What they were voting for was whatever served their own interests.

The *South Wales Argus* report was about as blunt as could be imagined: 'All we got was a whole series of clubs voting for what they perceived as their own interests. For example, those who felt threatened by the promise of automatic promotion voted in favour of the play-off system. Those who would be most affected by the ending of the semi-professional first division voted for that to continue. Those who had most to gain by the Sir Tasker Watkins working party report voted in favour of that. And those most worried that their funds would be cut off altogether voted for a continuance. At the same time, WRU top brass, who stood to lose the most by the implementation of the Watkins proposals, urged delegates to vote against that. It was all blatant self-interest with no-one prepared to really take the bull by the horns and vote for real change.'[31]

That self-interest included the wishes of somebody just off a nightshift who, way into a six-hour meeting, announced that he had another shift to go to and that a decision, any decision, needed to be reached. Phil Bowen, of Seven Sisters RFC, declared that – given his work commitments – he would go against the mandate he had been given by his club and would vote for the alternative Griffiths plan. He persuaded enough of his fellow delegates to do likewise and Griffiths' alternative proposals were passed.

Mike Hill, of Llantwit Major, was furious: 'I don't know why we bother. I agree with what Bridgend benefactor Leighton Samuel said recently. He is absolutely right in that 230 amateurs cannot vote on a professional game. The EGM was a good example of a case for taking the vote off clubs because they have not got a clue what they are talking about.'[32]

Arwyn Owen, editor of the *Welsh Brewers/Buy as You View Rugby Annuals* for Wales, summed up the general mood in his report on the vote: 'It is ludicrous that the small clubs possess the power to decide how the professional game should be run when it does not impact upon them.'[33]

One of Welsh rugby's greatest, Gerald Davies, wrote of his disillusionment the following day: '... there can be no conclusion other than that the general committee has simply given its version of the Harvey Smith salute to its own working party. This sorry tale serves to illuminate what appears to be a lack of principle. With no internal coherence, which this attitude suggests, what hope can there be for a future strategy to revive the sport at national and international level in Wales?'[34]

It would not be the last time that Gerald would feel compelled to criticise the administrators of his beloved sport.

CHAPTER 4

Rise of the Regionalists

'If Aneurin Bevan said that "politics in Westminster is in its infancy compared to Welsh rugby", then what the Welsh game needs... is statesmen. Welsh rugby needs a statesmanlike vision of a future with noble ambitions, fundamental to restoring its reputation and not one that has hitherto simply manifested the bar-room squabbling of parish-pump politicians.'[1]

(Gerald Davies, 'After years of neglect, the game is almost up for sorry Wales', *The Times*, 21 February 2003)

RELATIONS BETWEEN THE clubs and the WRU were at an all-time low in the summer of 2002. Swansea backers Mike James and Rob Davies were unequivocal: 'The only thing that has stopped us from pulling the plug is the delight the union would take in the club's downfall, and the responsibility we feel towards the players and, especially, the community of Swansea... Welsh rugby seems to encourage mediocrity at almost every level... The whole situation in Welsh rugby is an absolute disgrace.'[2]

A cursory look at the make-up of the WRU general committee at that time would have terrified the casual supporter. The *Welsh Mirror* ran a piece on its membership, their rugby experience and their views on their roles and the wider game. Among the many highlights were comments by Selwyn Walters who averred that, 'I always go along with the official press releases from the union – it's always been a policy of mine never to go into detail about anything really.' Ninety-three-year-old Ken Harris added, 'I am a life member, whatever that means. As such I feel I have a duty not to comment on the WRU, but I haven't voted in the last seven years.' John Jones insisted that 'everything in the garden would be rosy if the national side were as successful as others in the Six Nations,' which, while probably true, was kind of the point of the unrest. Terry Vaux, meanwhile, was keen to remind the reader of how lucky the WRU was to have him on board, since, 'if I was charging full professional fees, it would be enormously expensive for the game.'[3]

Nevertheless, the May EGM had agreed to some changes.

Rather than the eight-strong, independently appointed executive board, headed by a non-executive chairman, there would be a six-strong executive, but under the direction of a 19-strong board appointed by the clubs. Instead of focusing all player payments on the elite level, the second tier would remain semi-professional.

The WRU set up a steering group to oversee the changes and – in as deadpan a line as you could wish to read by Andy Howell in the *Western Mail* – 'resisted the temptation to co-opt independent people onto the steering group. Instead, it has set up a five-strong body composed entirely of general committee members'.[4] Glanmor Griffiths – now chairman and treasurer of the WRU and chair of Millennium Stadium PLC – was one of the five.

Fans of special or emergency general meetings – of which there had already been two by May 2002 – were in luck. Aberavon were threatening yet another, this time over their non-promotion from Division 1 to the then Welsh-Scottish league having won their championship twice in two years. The date set would be 20 July. The EGM went ahead, after the July annual general meeting and Aberavon lost. They were furious – but not with the clubs – saying that they had lost faith in the WRU's general committee and its running of the game.[5]

Little wonder. The AGM had exposed deep dissatisfaction with the WRU. It emerged that the WRU did not yet fully own the entirety of the site on which the Millennium Stadium had been built. Russell Jenkins of Cardiff HSOB criticised the 'total mismanagement of financial affairs in the last five years... We are in a disastrous position and I would suggest that you and the rest of the general committee should consider their positions and resign from running this union.'[6]

Glanmor Griffiths' response was not entirely conciliatory: 'It's people like you who do far more damage than anyone to our rapport with the moneymen by making these sorts of statements in public and scaremongering.'[7]

Meanwhile, Barclays Bank – owed around £60m by the WRU, the bulk of which had been incurred in building the Millennium Stadium and which cost nearly £4m a year in interest payments – installed its own experts to supervise the day-to-day running of the WRU and to implement cuts.[8] The WRU admitted that it would not be in a position to repay Barclays in the event that the bank decided to call in its debt. The union's annual income at this point stood at around £27m, with total debts at around £70m.

At this stage, the nine premier division clubs were sharing £8.1m each year, while the first division clubs received £90,000 each. National team coaches – past and present – were costing significant amounts, while the WRU's largesse extended to generating £900,000 of the total £1m television deal for the Celtic League and then putting it all into the overall costs of the sponsorless competition. The Welsh league remained unsponsored and the WRU was also struggling to find a shirt sponsor.[9] Test players' win bonuses were cut from £5,000 to £3,000; appearance fees were cut from up to £4,000 per game for the most experienced to a flat £1,000. Every club in the top division had been given a £200,000 loan when the game went professional which remained unpaid, and around £400,000 in Rugby World Cup 1999 ticket sales remained uncollected.[10] Again, player salaries came in for criticism, with WRU sources suggesting that they were too high.

There now came yet another threat of yet another EGM – this time led by Porthcawl. They had been denied promotion from Division Seven West due to a points deduction for having cancelled a game when they could not field a front-row of specialists. In a sign of where the balance of power lay within the Welsh game, Porthcawl brushed off criticism by Leighton Samuel, Bridgend's benefactor: 'Samuel was a member of the Gang of Six who attempted to hijack WRU money for their own needs. But he should remember what happened at the EGM it called.'[11]

This EGM – which would have been the fourth in five months – didn't go ahead.

The policy of rewarding on-field success with additional funding, which by definition would widen the financial gap between the professional clubs, had by now created a situation where clubs such as Ebbw Vale were receiving around £600,000 in annual payments from the WRU,[12] while clubs at the top were receiving over £1m. Ray Harris at Eugene Cross Park worried that the club could fold. The season's structure didn't help – Ebbw Vale faced a near four-month gap in their fixture list for the 2002–03 season in which they would have no home league matches. They had asked the WRU to step in by buying shares worth around £350,000, in addition to the approximately £240,000-worth the union already held. The union refused. Ebbw Vale called foul, pointing out that the WRU already fully owned Neath through Gower Park and held shares worth £705,000 in Swansea and £500,000 in Llanelli (in addition to owning Stradey Park). Caerphilly's director of rugby Gordon Pritchard resigned, praising his club's frugal approach: 'Caerphilly is a club who doesn't go moaning and groaning to the union every time they have a cash problem. They do everything within their budget and suffer because of it. If everyone did that, maybe the game would move forward. They deserve a fair crack of the whip.'[13]

Pritchard was the third senior member of Caerphilly's technical staff to leave mid-season, following coaches Terry Holmes and Charlie Faulkner's resignations earlier in the year.

Aberavon now threatened a civil case against the WRU, which might not go ahead if Ebbw Vale went to the wall and Aberavon were to replace them in the top-flight. Which might mean the end of the loyalty agreement which guaranteed eight clubs in the top-flight until 2007. Which in turn could allow the WRU to reduce the number of clubs without penalty.

In the midst of the chaos, Glanmor Griffiths was rewarded with a sixth successive term as WRU chairman. He had also by that point been honorary treasurer for 19 years and remained chairman of Millennium Stadium plc.

As the start of the 2002–03 season neared, a truce was declared between the WRU, the national team and the leading clubs. It took the form of an agreement – at an aspirational level, at least – that Test players should play no more than 20 club games per season. In return, more than 70 players were awarded dual contracts, in which the WRU undertook to pay, directly to their employing clubs, a proportion of their salary costs. This ranged from under £10,000 for Under-19 players to £40,000 for established Test stars.[14]

After losing 19 of 21 matches to Irish teams in 2001–02, the new Celtic League season began in familiar fashion as Welsh clubs lost all three matches against Irish opposition on the opening weekend. Worse, even Scottish teams now held the whip hand, with Glasgow winning in Cardiff and Edinburgh beating Swansea in the Scottish capital.

Rob Howley, who had retired from the national team at the end of the previous season's Six Nations and had left Cardiff for Wasps, was critical of player standards in Wales. He felt that, in comparison with standards at English clubs, he had been operating almost at a semi-professional level.[15] The gulf between union payments to clubs in England and Wales became ever more apparent. While the 12 English Zurich Premiership clubs received a flat £2.3m per club from the RFU, the Welsh sliding scale saw the Heineken Cup clubs receiving between £962,000 and £1.17m, while the teams in the second-tier European tournament received between £827,000 and just £530,000.[16] Mike Ruddock, at Ebbw Vale, called for the creation of two flat bands, with clubs in the Heineken Cup receiving one flat rate and teams in the second-tier competitions getting a separate, reduced flat rate, arguing that every top-division club needed to be able to afford at least 25 fully professional players.

Bridgend owner Leighton Samuel, whose team were by then being penalised by the system, felt that there was justification: 'When you finish seventh in the league you would want equal funding. If you finished top, you would not. It is all about self-preservation. The bottom line is the WRU is not doing anything for anybody. There are reasons for the difference in funding which I can understand. The premier clubs voted for this.'[17]

He went on to say that: 'The Gang of Six tried to force change and failed and Sir Tasker Watkins tried to do something and failed. It seems the system cannot be beaten.'[18]

The Heineken Cup went badly. Excluding Llanelli – who won five out of six pool matches before an early Dafydd Jones red card saw Perpignan triumph at Stradey in the quarter-finals – Cardiff, Swansea, Newport and Neath managed five wins between them in 24 matches.

The 16-team Celtic League saw a small improvement. In the eight-team Pool A, Neath were the sole Welsh qualifiers, mainly because only three of the eight teams were not Welsh and four had to progress. Pool B was a little better, with Pontypridd winning six out of seven to top the pool while Cardiff qualified in third place. Neath's path to the final involved two all-Welsh affairs, in which they beat Pontypridd and Cardiff before succumbing to a rampant Munster in the final.

Beneath the professional tier, the community game was crumbling. Blaenau Gwent RFC had been forced to cancel games, claiming that players were demanding payment for playing – in Division Seven East – and were decamping to other clubs when the club demurred.[19] Gwyn Jones confirmed that the situation was little better out west, with Loughor, Gorseinon and Pontarddulais struggling to raise teams.[20] The situation in the Swansea, Neath and Afan valleys was just as bad, with only one youth team running in the whole of the Swansea Valley and several teams disbanding in the Afan Valley.[21] At all levels and in all sports, participation in Wales was in freefall, but rugby appeared to be suffering more than most. By 1999, rugby was the ninth most popular participation sport in Wales among males, with just 4.3% of the population playing the game, way behind football which was played by 10% of adult males. It did not feature at all in the top ten for the female or overall populations.[22]

With discontent at all levels, the long-awaited establishment of a professional executive – initially in the form of new group chief executive officer David Moffett – set Welsh rugby on a reforming course. Moffett had been involved in amalgamating traditional clubs in the National Rugby League, had been there at the birth of professionalism and was involved in the creation of the Super Rugby provinces in New Zealand. He was amazed by what he found. 'When I got to Wales in 2002, it quickly became plain to me that the Welsh were living in the past. All the past glories were all they ever talked about. And they were completely unprepared for professional rugby. I arrived to a situation in which the Welsh Rugby Union was trading whilst insolvent. They had lost £3m the year I arrived and the professional game was an absolute mess. The biggest issue was the debt. When I got there it was about £72m.'

Moffett sat down with his board for the first time, ready to tackle the situation he had inherited: 'I can remember sitting at my first meeting of the board and this guy said to me – and I'll never forget this – "David, I notice that a couple of the jerseys got ripped on the weekend. Can you tell me what you're going to do about it?" And I'm sitting there and I've got this union which is trading whilst insolvent, £72m in debt, a team that's not winning and this guy's more interested in the fact that the jerseys ripped?'

Moffett's first task was to get to grips with the financial situation. He negotiated with Barclays (who had funded much of the loan which had been used to build the Millennium Stadium) and BT (who owned a portion of the land on which the new stadium stood and had never been paid).

'I told the board that I was going to renegotiate the debt, which is what I did, down to round about £45m. So, BT and the bank had to take a haircut and a decent haircut at that. And I set that up so that the place knew where it was going for the next 25 to 30 years.'

By 2004, the overall debt had been significantly reduced and was now payable over a longer term, which allowed the final £9m payment to be made to BT for the land on which the stadium's South Stand stood. The union now, at last, fully owned their stadium.

'I can remember one of the very first things I said, I think, at my first press conference, was that there was going to be some pain. I don't think people realised how much pain there was going to be. I got rid of a lot of people, pared us down to a very small number of people in the office, stopped all the freebies for the board members, stopped them from being able to take their wives on junkets at Welsh Rugby Union expense... That was low-hanging fruit and I could do that quite quickly and get some quite instantaneous results.'[23]

The big challenge was around the number of professional teams which Wales could sustain. After all, as Roger Blyth of Swansea recalled being asked by David Moffett: 'Well, you have nine professional clubs in Wales. How many are there in South Africa? Australia? New Zealand? And you want nine?!'[24]

Moffett's initial preference was said to be for five teams, based on existing clubs at Newport, Cardiff, Pontypridd, Swansea and Llanelli.[25] Terry Cobner favoured four geographical regions.[26] Others threw their ideas into the ring. Graham Price followed his former Pontypool colleague in favouring four new provinces or regions. Gareth Jenkins at Llanelli believed that regions would represent 'nowhere and nobody' and favoured five franchised teams which could be either stand-alone clubs or amalgamations. Stephen Jones, in the *Sunday Times*, wrote: 'The fatal error now would be to abandon the professional club game because it has failed, when the truth is that, because of the lack of support and funding from the WRU, it has never really been tried.'[27] Mike Burton suggested five super clubs based in Llanelli, Swansea, Cardiff, Newport and the vaguely-defined 'Valleys'.[28]

There were voices which felt that it may already have been too late, such as Stephen Jones: 'It is a sobering thought indeed that if what is needed happens immediately (WRU resignations today, professional directorate today, reduction of professional teams today, elitism today, professionalism today), then it may already be too late. As recent history has found, to have a workable plan for an elite is one thing. To get it past the grim ranks of the petty jealous is another.'[29]

With discussions seemingly moving towards four regions or five super clubs, a significant spanner was thrown into the works with the news that Neath and Bridgend – in a hitherto unheard-of proposal, but apparently with the WRU's blessing (who, after all, owned Neath) – were pursuing a tie-up for European and Celtic League competition.[30]

And then, the bombshell. David Moffett announced his favoured option. There would be four regions, employing no more than 150 players in total, based in Llanelli, Cardiff, Newport and, out of left field, Wrexham.

One, unnamed, club official, quoted in the *Mirror*, was: 'gobsmacked... there was praise for the lead taken by Neath and Bridgend in suggesting a merger and then all of a sudden a completely different plan for provincial rugby was whipped out... the simple fact is that provincial rugby is not attractive to anyone except the union.'[31]

Alun Carter and Nick Bishop later wrote: 'Some of Moffett's initial ideas, which included the cultivation of north Wales as a new playing resource, showed what a double-edged sword his appointment could turn out to be. While he was refreshingly free of the 'village-isms' that beset those in Wales, he had a grasp of Welsh rugby geography that was at times childish in outlook.'[32]

Recriminations followed. Llanelli's Stuart Gallacher suspected that the WRU – owners of Neath through Gower Park – had misled the other clubs. Mike Cuddy, at Neath, criticised the 'self-interest' of Llanelli.[33]

The clubs responded with two proposals of their own. Both meant five teams, with mergers between Newport and Ebbw Vale, and Cardiff and Caerphilly, constants in both. In one model, Pontypridd stood alone, Llanelli and Swansea would merge, as would Neath and Bridgend. In the other, Llanelli stood alone, while Swansea and Neath would merge, with Bridgend and Pontypridd forming a Mid Glamorgan-based team.[34]

Agreement was hard to reach. A meeting between the premier division clubs and the WRU, scheduled for 12 December, was cancelled as the clubs could not finalise their proposals.[35]

By January 2003, Moffett – seeing no possibility of pushing through a model which included a north Wales region –

downgraded the proposal for a northern region (albeit there was suspicion that his initial proposal hadn't been entirely serious and was intended to shock the clubs into action).[36] There would now be four regions in the south and – with £8m available – each of the four would receive payments of £2m each from the WRU, with a development region in the north. It appeared that the Neath/Bridgend and Newport/Ebbw Vale mergers were agreed. The sticking points now were the status of the teams in the west, with Llanelli and Swansea resistant to partnering with each other, and in the central belt, where a proposed Cardiff/Pontypridd/Caerphilly tie-up was proving to be equally indigestible.[37]

One more acrimonious meeting break-up later and, within a week, the clubs were back with more proposals. In addition to the Llanelli/Swansea, Neath/Bridgend, Cardiff/Pontypridd and Newport/Ebbw Vale proposal, they now had a new plan. Newport and Ebbw Vale's partnership remained, but now Cardiff and Llanelli would stand alone, Swansea would join with Neath, and Bridgend with Pontypridd.[38] Llanelli were fully aware of the financial impact of the second of these proposals – clubs who opted to stand-alone would receive smaller payments from the WRU. The £1.3m which any stand-alone would receive – merged clubs would receive £1.8m – was scarcely more than they already got.[39]

The WRU board now met and decided on four regional sides, based on formally tendered-for franchises, all in the south. Moffett wanted to see 'a true partnership with the WRU – all 239 clubs, not two, three or nine'. However, he was open to single or combined club tenders and accepted that benefactors who had pumped so much money into the Welsh game would continue to be essential.[40]

The reaction of the clubs was mixed. Swansea's Roger Blyth indicated a willingness to consider a merger with Llanelli, provided it was a true 50/50 partnership, with games played both at Stradey Park and at St Helen's. Pontypridd's chief executive Gareth Thomas felt that the geographical element of the proposed regions militated against his club's chances, claiming that, 'the way this has been put together, it is designed so that certain individual clubs will win the franchises... if we fail to be a successful bidder... we [will] have to seek legal advice accordingly'. Neath's Mike Cuddy was supportive of the four-region plan which included a Neath/Bridgend merger. Leighton Samuel agreed, noting that the number of players and available finances pushed a four-team solution, with Bridgend willing to consider mergers with either Neath or Pontypridd.[41]

Between the need for external, non-WRU-generated money and the existing loyalty agreements which still had five years to run, it was becoming clear that the WRU did not have the ability to force through its preferred model. It would need to reach agreement with the top clubs and would then need to secure the agreement of the majority of its member clubs to any new structure.

By the end of the month, Cardiff and Llanelli continued to push for stand-alone status. Leighton Samuel was furious at the suggestion that two clubs should remain unscathed while others merged, and even angrier at suggestions that his club might merge with both Neath and Pontypridd to ensure that they could.[42]

Given the significance of the proposed changes, an emergency general meeting of the full WRU membership would be required. The date was set for 23 February. Six of the eight clubs now seemed to support the WRU's preferred four-team model. Cardiff may also have been coming around to the notion of a partnership with Pontypridd, but, given Cardiff Athletic Club rules around the identity of teams which could use the Arms Park and Lynn Howells later repeat of a fan's 'quip' that, 'if his team joined Cardiff and happened to be playing on his back lawn, he still wouldn't draw back the curtains to watch them',[43] this appeared to have limited potential. Plans for franchises were rejected, as the legal complexities of getting such a decision through the EGM made them unworkable. These would be voluntary mergers between existing clubs, with playing staff jointly contracted to the new teams and the WRU, with the possibility of players' drafts which could move players around the new teams at the WRU's behest.[44]

The resolution put to the EGM was deliberately vague, noting that the union would support: 'the establishment of new regionally-based organisations to participate in the Celtic League and European Rugby Cup Ltd competitions and such other competitions as the board of directors may from time to time consider appropriate.'[45]

In other words, the proposition put before the clubs – and which they eventually supported by an overwhelming 408 votes to seven – was for a smaller number of teams, 'regionally-based', to be put forward by the WRU for cross-border competition. Crucially, it did not specify a number of teams. Nor did it specify that these would be regions, merely 'regionally-based'. The door remained open to regions, super clubs, mergers, or a mishmash of all three.

Llanelli – in its desire to stand alone – had threatened to request an injunction against the WRU to prevent it from ripping up the loyalty agreements which guaranteed its place, as a club, at the top table until at least 2007. By issuing the injunction in March, with the courts unable to consider the merits of the case until May, they would force the WRU to miss a 2 April deadline set by Heineken Cup officials for the submission of the names of the WRU's entrants in European tournaments the following season.[46]

'The WRU knows this proposal is not viable,' Llanelli's chief executive, Stuart Gallacher, said. 'It admits to blockages with the European Rugby Cup and broadcasters and we, along with other clubs, have made clear our intention to take legal action if they persisted. We are not against change but if the union do not face up to the fact that their option is dead in the water and pursue other options, we will miss the 2 April deadline that ERC have given us to come up with a structure for next season's Heineken Cup. We will be stuck with nine clubs and nobody wants that. The four-team regional plan would put Llanelli out of business and we will not allow that to happen. We have a duty, not to mention contractual obligations to our players, staff and suppliers and to our members, shareholders and supporters. Unlike the WRU, we take our legal and moral obligations seriously.'[47]

Ron Jones felt that there was a more fundamental reason for Llanelli's insistence on standing alone. Back in 1997, when he had joined with others to save the club and had been appointed chair, he had told supporters: 'We will play, as Llanelli, as the Scarlets, at the highest level of European rugby, or nothing. We knew that we couldn't deliver it [a merger]. If the proposal to stay independent had failed, we'd have gone to the wall, because we'd have gone back on promises we had made to supporters. The joke is that Cardiff, like us, were broke. It wasn't that we could do it financially. You were playing poker. Moffett says that we ruined the restructure by saying that we wouldn't join with anybody, but tough. We aren't here to make the union's life easier, we're here to protect our club and the special people who contribute within the community.'[48]

A few days later, Stephen Jones reported in the *Sunday Times* that a compromise set-up of five teams was close to being agreed. Approving of Llanelli's stubbornness, he applauded the reaffirmation of the importance of the club game: 'The decision to extend the domestic game to five clubs is a belated recognition that the whole of domestic rugby in any country does not exist simply for the single purpose of forming a national rugby team... Frankly, the fewer and shorter the central tentacles around the new game extended by the WRU, the better.' He went on to reject the very concept of provinces or regions: 'Rugby in Wales will always be based squarely on communities, not by drawing lines on a map.'[49]

Finally, on April Fool's Day 2003, David Moffett was able to announce a resolution. There would be five teams. Llanelli and Cardiff would stand alone and would receive reduced WRU payments of around £1.3m for their trouble. Neath would merge with Swansea, Bridgend with Pontypridd, and Newport with Ebbw Vale. The three merged teams would receive nearly £1.8m each.

In the near certainty that WRU payments to clubs in the tier below the new elite level would reduce from around £1m per club to closer to £50,000 under the new system, Swansea had already put themselves into voluntary administration the previous month. Most of their £2.5m debt was either owed to benefactors (who wrote off their significant investments) or to players who would transfer into the new system.[50] Nevertheless, players immediately faced cuts to their wages mid-season and several high-profile players – including Colin Charvis, Ben Evans and Darren Morris – were released with two months of the season still to be played.

'Professionalism has ruined Swansea and left the club where we are today,' said the club's director of rugby, Richard Moriarty.[51]

Elsewhere, the changes to the WRU's governance agreed over a year earlier were now implemented in full. Moffett now had his executive board in place. The general committee would be slimmed down from 28 to 19 members. There was no longer a role for Glanmor Griffiths – honorary treasurer since 1984, chairman of the general committee and of Millennium Stadium plc since 1997 – who finally stood down.[52]

His reign wasn't recalled with the greatest fondness by many in Welsh rugby. The former Cardiff number 8 John Scott, writing in his *South Wales Echo* column, was scathing: 'Griffiths... should have gone at least a couple of years ago. He did the game a disservice by campaigning against the

Sir Tasker Watkins reform project last year. He should have worked from within the working party he was originally a part of instead of touring the districts with his own hastily cobbled together plan... nothing more than a spoiler.'[53]

Perhaps the following David Moffett anecdote – on Glanmor Griffiths' decision to stand down – best sums up the calamitous chaos of Welsh rugby in the late 1990s and early 2000s, forever buffeted by events, never in control of its own destiny: 'Glanmor used to say quite often, I found out, that he thought he might leave because he'd done his time. That was really just to try to get people to say "Glan, don't go, you're too important." So, I did that on a couple of occasions and I said, "No, no, I don't think you should go." On the third occasion he said it to me I said, "Yeah, I think you'd better go." It was at a Six Nations game up in Scotland and I told all the board that Glanmor had told me that he wanted to go and that I thought he should. I don't think he ever meant it. But he'd never had somebody there who was prepared to call his bluff. And even as we walked into the board meeting where [David] Pickering was going to be anointed as the next chairman, Pickering was trying to talk him out of leaving.'[54]

CHAPTER 5

A New Year Nearing, Full of Relentless Surprises

'The Welsh are always at war with themselves.
And you can see it now. It's bizarre, because if they actually
stopped to think, and said, "You know, we're going to
actually unite, as Welsh people," they'd be special. But it's
never going to happen.'[1]

(David Moffett, in conversation with the author)

BETWEEN THE VARIOUS competing interests – the WRU's need
to cut costs, the national coaches' desire to see a reduction
in the number of teams, the desire of the Gang of Six to be
awarded elite status, the desire of the non-Gang-of-Six clubs
in the top two tiers to remain relevant, and the desire of many
of the other 230-odd Welsh clubs to bring everybody else
down a peg or two – a way forward had been found for the
elite game.

The end of the 2002–03 season had been something of a
damp squib.

Bridgend won their first league title; Leighton Samuel's
'crass' line that the cut-glass league trophy was 'the most

expensive vase I've ever bought' didn't impress Gareth Thomas.[2]

In the 13 years since formal leagues had been introduced, Swansea were the most successful in terms of league titles with four. Their western brethren in Llanelli (with three) and Neath (with two) were close behind, with Cardiff the only other club to triumph more than once. The overall playing record showed six clubs with a win-loss record of better than 50% – Cardiff led the way on 71%, followed by Swansea and Llanelli on 66%, Pontypridd and Neath on 64% and 63% respectively, and Bridgend just scraping into the positive on 51%.

Llanelli won their twelfth Cup. Of the 32 editions of the Challenge Cup held since its reintroduction in 1972, Llanelli and Cardiff – who themselves had won seven – had hoovered up 19 between them. Neath and Swansea were next in the list, with three each.

In European competition, Llanelli's defeat to Perpignan at the quarter-final stage brought the curtain down on the involvement of the old clubs, in their original form, in Europe's elite competition after eight seasons. They had been Wales' standard-bearers in the tournament, achieving a win-loss record of 68%, well ahead of Cardiff on 56%, Pontypridd on 43% and Swansea on 41%. Five quarter-finals had been reached, with two unsuccessful forays into the semi-finals. Cardiff had managed three quarter-finals, two semi-finals and one final, while Swansea had reached two knockout matches. Pontypridd were the only other club to have made it through the group stage, although that was in the 1998–99 season when no English clubs (nor Cardiff or Swansea) participated.

By the later stages, clubs not in contention for trophies allowed their leading players to leave for extended time with the national squad ahead of the autumn's Rugby World Cup in Australia.

World Cup preparations did not go well.

'More hated than Osama bin Laden!'[3] screamed the

headlines in February 2003. As Western governments prepared for war in Iraq – ostensibly in retaliation for the Al-Qaeda attacks of 9/11 – and millions marched in opposition to those plans, the subject of the Welsh public's ire, expressed in an opinion poll in the *Wales on Sunday*, was Wales captain Colin Charvis. His crime? In the opening 2003 Six Nations defeat in Rome, he had been substituted and had been seen to – and I hope you're sitting down to read this, dear reader – smile. That's right. The captain of Wales smiled while Wales were losing a game of rugby.

He may have taken some consolation from the fact that he was less hated than Saddam Hussein, but maybe not much.

A first whitewash of the Six Nations era – but a third in the championship in 13 years – followed. That summer, Wales visited Australia and New Zealand – a trip which almost didn't happen. Steve Lewis, newly-appointed as WRU CEO under group chief executive David Moffett, met with the players to deliver some harsh messages. The union had spent £5.6m on the Wales squad in the previous four seasons, said Lewis, with players receiving up to £217,000 in WRU payments in that time.[4]

Alun Carter recalls that fractious first meeting between Steve Lewis and the squad: 'Lewis gave a presentation in the lounge of the St Bride's Hotel, voicing many harsh truths in quite a confrontational manner. [He] made little attempt at diplomacy, telling the players bluntly that they were overpaid. "That's all going to change," he said, "You probably won't have the brain to understand the new system… except maybe for you, Mark Taylor."'[5]

On the day of departure for Australia, and with the bus waiting outside their Vale of Glamorgan base to take them to Heathrow, the players didn't show up. They were at a service station, refusing to get on the bus, until their issues with the proposed new pay structure had been resolved. They were eventually persuaded to embark – given the choice of that or the sack, they opted for the former – but they missed their scheduled flight. The players had to pay for their own overnight accommodation at an airport hotel and flew out on two separate flights – one via the USA, the other via Malaysia.

Once the team got on the field, matters didn't improve. A 30–10 defeat in Australia was followed by a 55–3 thumping by New Zealand. Once home, a strong Welsh team played a second-string English team in Cardiff and lost 43–9. A 23-point defeat in Dublin left coach Steve Hansen facing calls for his removal. His team then beat Romania and Scotland, and he was able to take the team to the Rugby World Cup. The first green shoots of recovery could be seen in the thrilling pool match against New Zealand and the quarter-final, in which Wales outscored eventual champions England by three tries to one before succumbing to the greater power of the English pack.

Back at home, David Moffett's cost-cutting continued. Fifty WRU staff were released, successful Wales A and age-grade teams were cut, along with women's teams.[6]

And then, in September 2003, the new elite structure made its bow.

The summer had been anything but trouble free, particularly over in the east, where the team had eventually settled on the name 'Gwent Dragons'.

Arguments continued. Newport RFC supporters weren't buying season tickets (just 1,000 having been sold by August). Neither were supporters from the rest of Gwent. By August, Ebbw Vale chairman Marcus Russell resigned as a director. The following day, Newport benefactor Tony Brown rejoined as a director and the team's name was changed to Newport Gwent Dragons.

'It's a shame it had to come to this, but unless urgent action was taken the region would have been bankrupt by Christmas. In order to avoid that Marcus Russell resigned and he appears to blame everyone but himself, so Newport had to step in and fill the void,' said Brown.[7]

Now it was Pontypridd's turn to go into administration with debts of £675,000,[8] £46,000 of which was owed to the Celtic Warriors, who had stepped in to cover the salary costs of Pontypridd's players the previous June. The region's chairman Leighton Samuel offered to pay £400,000 for Pontypridd's share of the Celtic Warriors. Pontypridd refused.

'I do not see how Pontypridd can remain partners with Bridgend in the Warriors; the last four months have been a nightmare. We struggled to make any decisions and it was only recently that I became aware of the extent of their financial problems,' said Samuel.

Samuel saw this as evidence of the feeble financial situation of Welsh rugby. He had long argued that it was only with significant benefactor input that professional rugby could survive, and this latest situation appeared to prove his point: 'What all this shows is that, if we had not gone down the regional route last summer, there would probably only be four solvent professional clubs in Wales: Bridgend, Newport, Cardiff and Llanelli, all of which have been kept going by benefactors... What has happened is sad and shows how hard it is to manage a club without a benefactor.'[9]

Pontypridd's success during the 1990s had been funded in large part by local company Buy As You View. Lynn Howells confirmed the club's dependency on their main sponsor: 'Buy As You View had been a great supporter of Pontypridd rugby for several years, but their financial commitment to the club was very different to the benefactors who supported the likes of Newport, Llanelli, and Cardiff. Buy As You View had their name on the shirts and if one of the players needed a car, it arrived with the company logo on it which helped the club, and they got their return from being associated with a successful local rugby team. Their financial commitment was more in kind than in hard cash. If Cardiff, Newport or Llanelli needed money, then Peter Thomas, Tony Brown or Huw Evans would reach into their pockets and pull out the cheque book. That didn't happen with Buy As You View.'[10]

Samuel eventually bought Pontypridd's 50% share from the administrators for around £100,000 and gifted it to the WRU.

With the situations at the Celtic Warriors and Newport Gwent Dragons appearing to have reached some kind of uneasy settlement, attention turned towards the new teams on the pitch. The improvement in playing standards was immediately obvious, with Welsh teams flying high in the Celtic League and competitive in Europe.

But by April, the Celtic Warriors were back in trouble. Chief executive Leighton Samuel resigned, announcing that his financial backing would be withdrawn by the end of May. In a statement released on the Warriors' website, he declared that he had put £1m of his own money into the region (in addition to several million spent on Bridgend).

WRU CEO David Moffett was deeply unimpressed: 'I would have thought it would have been good to at least have had a discussion with them. I'm extremely disappointed that such a serious and significant statement, with obviously far-reaching consequences, was made to the media before it was discussed at board level.'[11]

The scale of the problem was perhaps not surprising, given Samuel's investment. He had sanctioned the assembling of a very expensive squad, with senior players including Gareth Thomas and Dafydd James said to be earning in excess of £100,000 a year.

'The squad costs were horrendous,' recalled Lynn Howells. 'As their share of the WRU funding each month, the Warriors would receive £137,500, but the wage bill alone was £200,000. Also, the WRU money arrived in the club's bank early in the month, but the salaries went out one month in arrears, so there was always a scramble to cash the cheques in case the money ran out.'[12]

Samuel's withdrawal appeared to be at least partly caused by an argument over the previous week's Celtic League game with Munster, which, in a departure from the norm by this stage, had been taken to Pontypridd's Sardis Road ground. The media reported a crowd of 5,500, Samuel insisted there were 4,157 present, and Samuel was accused by some of massaging the figure downwards for tax reasons. He was not best pleased.

The *Western Mail* reported that it was now hard to see how the Warriors could survive into the following season.

By May, those fears had been realised. A review of the regions' finances, instigated by the WRU in April, was the final straw and led – according to Lynn Howells – to Leighton Samuel seeking a way out. He sold his half of the region to the WRU, claiming that he had received assurances that the WRU would support its continuation into the following season. Within days it was announced that the region would fold. It later emerged that the WRU – unable to raise the required £1.25m required to buy out Samuel's share – had instead asked the other four regions to contribute, which they did to the tune of £312,500 each.

The reaction across Wales was one of sadness, and of concern at the removal of elite rugby from the former Mid Glamorgan county area. J.J. Williams, who had himself played at Bridgend, blamed the WRU: 'I don't think David Moffett understands what Welsh rugby is all about,' he told the BBC.[13]

By 1 June, the Celtic Warriors were put into liquidation by the Welsh Rugby Union and officially consigned to the history books.[14]

In their one season, they had finished fourth in the Celtic League, winning 17 of their 28 Celtic League games, bowing out at the group stage of the European Cup after a memorable victory over eventual champions Wasps in High Wycombe.

Ultimately, their demise was caused by a lack of money.

Samuel himself projected a £500,000 loss in the first season, which he had initially indicated he was willing to make up. Since his first major involvement with Bridgend in 1999, it was claimed that he had thrown £4m into professional rugby in Wales.

Gareth Thomas recalled the financial chaos which enveloped the region: '[the] Celtic Warriors [was] a regional franchise that expired because of a lack of strategic support from the WRU. They felt it was not financially viable – hardly a surprise to me, given that Jemma and I had to take out a loan to cover our mortgage payments when pay cheques bounced. Less fortunate team-mates were treated disgracefully – like cattle at an auction.'[15]

The Warriors needed big crowds to make up the shortfall, but they didn't appear. In fact, their crowds were the sparsest of the five regions – averaging 3,327 across all competitions. The Ospreys were little better at 3,553, while Cardiff Blues attracted average attendances of 4,856, the Dragons 5,288 and the Scarlets – who won the league – 9,098. Even local derbies didn't bring them in – the game against the Ospreys at the Brewery Field was played in front of just 2,500 people, while the Dragons game had been played at Sardis Road in front of just 1,477 supporters.[16] With Samuel gone, they had no benefactor to cover their losses.

Ron Jones, watching from Llanelli as events unfolded in Mid Glamorgan, felt that Samuel hadn't grasped the scale of the investment required to make a region work: 'He'd misunderstood, I think, how much money you needed to put in to keep the professional game going. The boys at Liberty were at the Ospreys, you had Huw Evans with us, you had plenty of money at that time in Cardiff… Cardiff Athletic Club still putting money in, a few very wealthy people at the Dragons. But Leighton was on his own, and he could never have kept paying out that kind of money.'[17]

David Moffett added: 'Celtic Warriors wound themselves

up. We [WRU] had no money, so we couldn't help anybody. Pontypridd were broke and went into administration. At the Brewery Field they were getting crowds of around 1,500 and Leighton Samuel, the owner, said he wasn't going to continue. So, it was market forces. It was a sad day, but five teams was most likely too many.'[18]

On the field, the concentration to a smaller number of teams appeared to have worked. Five of the top six spots in the final Celtic League table were occupied by the Welsh regions. Standards were noticeably higher. Wales' professional teams were competitive.

Terry Cobner, stepping down from his role as the WRU director of rugby, called for a dose of reality: 'My one wish now would be to see the clubs and players in Wales accept that we have two games now – a very limited professional game in four regions and a community game that encompasses the bulk of the clubs.'[19]

By September 2004, three of the regions had agreed a new participation agreement with the WRU. It would be far-ranging – giving the WRU a say in the appointment of regional coaches, training, dietary and nutritional issues, plus regulations on the recruitment of foreign players in the future and in which tournaments the regions would play. The Dragons signed in December 2004.

At Test level, the Welsh team suddenly, and rather unexpectedly, took flight. At least, it was unexpected to most supporters, notwithstanding the fleeting glimpses of excellence at the previous year's Rugby World Cup. Steve Hansen had left for New Zealand in the summer of 2004, reuniting within the All Blacks coaching team with the man who had brought him to Wales, Graham Henry.

One man who was perhaps a little less surprised by the sudden toughening up of the national team was new head coach Mike Ruddock, who, according to analyst Alun Carter, had long felt that fitness and conditioning weren't major problems in Welsh representative rugby, rather the fundamentals of forward play weren't sufficiently prioritised by the Test team. After all, Wales A won four from five and the Under-21s won the championship while the senior team were being whitewashed in 2003.[20]

Ruddock may have been the union's last-minute choice over Gareth Jenkins, but he was not in a strong enough position to choose his own assistants. He would be expected to inherit most of Hansen's remaining coaching ticket. Clive Griffiths was the only one of his assistants he was permitted to appoint.

Trailing the Springboks by 23–6 early on in their first significant test of the autumn of 2004, they twice reeled in their opponents with rare verve, eventually succumbing by just two points in a 38–36 thriller. Two weeks later, Wales came closer to beating the All Blacks than they had – and still, to this point, have – since 1978. The stadium clock had been switched – apparently unknown to the players – to actual game time. At 76 minutes, Wales – four points down – were awarded a penalty. They kicked the points to reduce the deficit to one. When the clock ticked over 80 minutes, Wales assumed that there was injury time to come, and Stephen Jones poked a kick into touch outside the New Zealand 22. The referee blew for full-time. Amid scenes of confusion, Wales had lost 25–26.

That All Blacks team went on to eviscerate France in Paris the following week. A chance missed for Wales, but they appeared to be in good shape.

The Six Nations of 2005 was glorious, a first Grand Slam in 27 years secured in the most thrilling, swashbuckling of styles. A scruffy win over England in the first game in Cardiff was followed by a comfortable victory in Rome. In Paris, Wales were battered, pulled from pillar to post, and yet they held on. Two quick tries early in the second half turned a hopeless cause into a hopeful one. A heroic rearguard effort saw the team home before the shackles were released in Murrayfield.

Wales scored six tries in an astonishing performance. A March Saturday in Cardiff, imported from high summer, saw Wales charge to the Grand Slam with an emphatic victory over Ireland.

Domestically, the Ospreys made it two Welsh champions in two seasons in the Celtic League. After a difficult first season for the West Glamorgan region, everything seemed to click. Several 10,000-plus crowds turned out to watch the team, doubling their average attendance on the previous season. Replica jersey sales increased to 38,000, making the Ospreys jersey the second highest-selling club jersey in Britain and Ireland, behind Munster. By the end of their championship winning season, they had made a profit of around £300,000.

The Ospreys, celebrating their commercial and on-field success, were unequivocal: 'We want to be in a position where if ever a European league, or a Euro-12 type competition came into existence, the Ospreys would be one of the first names suggested as a member club.[21]

Financially, the game was much more stable. So much so that the Scarlets were able to buy back Stradey Park from the WRU, to whom they had sold the famous old stadium eight years earlier. They needed the land on which Stradey stood to help finance a new stadium on the outskirts of the town.

Recruitment stepped up, as genuine world stars began appearing for the Welsh regions. The statement signing of 2005 was that of Jonah Lomu – past his best, maybe, but his presence filled Cardiff Arms Park several times over the course of the season. The Ospreys would arguably outdo that bit of business the following season, recruiting the New Zealand duo of Justin Marshall and Filo Tiatia, and later Jerry Collins and Marty Holah.

And yet, in the wild world of Welsh rugby, such contentment and stability could not last.

Welsh supporters had bridled at the dismissiveness of much of the English rugby firmament. There were insinuations in the London media that Wales' Grand Slam was 'built on sand'. Clive Woodward, leading the Lions to New Zealand, praised his Welsh players to the hilt and then picked hardly any of them for the first Test. When his plan of wrapping every English Rugby World Cup-winning player in cotton wool for the tour before letting them loose in that first Test fell apart, he threw some of the Welsh players a bone. It was too late.

Then, in October 2005, David Moffett announced that he would resign as the WRU's CEO. He left with a parting shot: 'The answer for us is central contracting. It's not something we're trying to do to help the Welsh Rugby Union, it's a matter of doing what's best for the country with a small player base. Maybe we'll see it introduced when the so-called benefactors get sick of losing money.'[22]

Reactions to the departure of this divisive figure were appropriately all over the place. The north Wales *Daily Post* declared him Wales' 'greatest Grand Slam hero… who got every minute detail right off the pitch'.[23] Lynn Howells, meanwhile, declared Moffett to be 'one of the most ignorant men I have ever met'.[24]

I guess you can't please all the people all the time.

Moffett has often expressed his regret at not having been able to push through his desired model: 'To make regional rugby work, I needed to go the next step, which was to create proper regions. Get rid of the districts, and just have four regions that had a team as part of their district, if you like, but only four of them. But I couldn't be bothered with the fight any longer. So, I decided that I'd leave. And I regretted leaving quite often afterwards because I enjoy the cut and thrust of that stuff.'[25]

Huw Jones felt that there wasn't much more Moffett could have achieved at that time: 'I think that was about as far as he could get, and he wouldn't have got anywhere at all if he'd tried to push further. It would have been a house of cards, it would all have fallen, and we'd have landed up with the same number of teams in the premier division, and they would all have been professional, and we'd have just carried on as we were. And everybody would have eventually gone bust.'[26]

The November 2005 match with New Zealand was billed as an unofficial world championship match. The northern hemisphere's Grand Slam champions against the southern hemisphere's Lions-slaying Tri-Nations champions. Held in part to mark the centenary of the first-ever game between the two nations in 1905, Wales were resoundingly thrashed.

As 2005 rolled into 2006, a first win over Australia since 1987 was welcome, but the opening of the Six Nations at Twickenham was ugly. Overpowered Wales succumbed 47–13. Lee Byrne recalls what happened as the bus took the team back to their base for the weekend: 'As the coach pulled up at the hotel in Richmond, Mike [Ruddock] asked the players not to go out that night. With that, he got off the bus, at which point a senior player stood up and told the driver to take us into London anyway. Poor Mike was left to walk alone into the hotel.'[27]

Among the players heading out for the night was the captain, Gareth Thomas. 'I went to our team manager, Alan Phillips, and told him that a posse of our players, me included, were planning on heading into London that night, but that even though I was intending to go, I did not think it was a particularly good idea.'

Alun Carter and Nick Bishop couldn't understand why, if the captain thought going out on the town was such a bad idea, he intended on joining his team-mates.[28]

There were clear tensions within the camp, with Gareth Thomas insisting on the removal of Graham Thomas – a journalist who had ghosted Gavin Henson's *My Grand Slam Year*, chronicling the centre's experiences over the previous twelve months – from a Wales press conference in the run-up to the following weekend's clash with Scotland. There were rumours of resentment among some senior players that coach

Mike Ruddock had, they felt, taken too much of the credit for the Grand Slam the previous season. Adam Jones, in his autobiography *Bomb*, revealed that: 'There had been a continuous backdrop of sniping. Certain senior players who'd bonded with the previous regime constantly questioned Mike's methods, undermined his authority, and made things awkward. Among the chief detractors were Gareth Thomas, Martyn Williams, Stephen Jones, and Brent Cockbain. I'm not saying these guys were especially disruptive or manipulative, but it was clear they were still in thrall to Hansen and Johnson. I'm pretty sure they liked Mike as a bloke, but they didn't rate him as a coach. Those players I've mentioned weren't actively trying to start a revolution, but they'd ask you what you thought about certain sessions. "Did you think they were effective? Were they worthwhile?" With every negative thought, and every question raised, they were chipping away at the foundations. The cracks grew wider, and those foundations eventually started to crumble.'[29]

Indeed, senior players were meeting with Steve Lewis, without Ruddock's knowledge. The content of those meetings remains the subject of conjecture, although Gareth Thomas insists that the main issue in the week of the Scotland game had been about player insurance, and his concern that two players were being asked to play while the status of their insurance was uncertain.[30]

Some of the coaching team weren't entirely onside, either. And, it later emerged, Ruddock had never actually signed a contract for his role as head coach. It remained, unsigned, in draft form.

There were three major issues with the draft contract as far as Ruddock was concerned. Firstly, WRU CEO Steve Lewis had the final say on team selection, not Ruddock as head coach. Secondly, there was no independent grievance procedure – Lewis would be the final arbiter. And thirdly, while Ruddock's contract specified that all contracted coaches should report directly to him, neither of his assistants – Scott Johnson and Clive Griffiths – had signed contracts either.[31]

Even so, Scotland were seen off, a red card for Scott Murray early in the game paving the way for a comfortable Welsh win.

Three days later, the *Western Mail* were preparing to run a story that coach Mike Ruddock – eleven months on from securing that first Grand Slam in more than a quarter of a century – was to step down. Andy Howell, at the *Western Mail*, had received a letter, purporting to have been sent to him by a member of the playing squad, saying that the players wanted Ruddock to go.

It may be difficult to imagine today, but the newspaper's intention was to spend the day developing the story and then to run an exclusive in the following morning's paper edition. However, throughout the day, more and more rumours leaked out. Ruddock and Lewis met and agreed that Ruddock would see out the season and leave in the summer. Ruddock had a press release, prepared by Andy Howell, ready to go. But then the WRU informed Ruddock that he was to leave with immediate effect, that he was not to turn up for work the next day, and that a press conference would be called for 9pm that evening to make the announcement. Ruddock was devastated.

An internal WRU memo was left in full sight of journalists at the press briefing, which outlined the union's desperation to 'control the story': 'We are in a situation where Mike is set to go, Scott Johnson is thought to be on the verge of returning to Australia and Clive Griffiths does not have a contract. There is only one interpretation of these facts – chaos and poor management.'[32]

While Steve Lewis and David Pickering, as CEO and chairman, set out on their 'Red Zone Roadshows' with the intention of explaining away the apparent chaos, they sent their captain to appear on the BBC Wales *Scrum V* programme for a now-infamous set-to. Wearing the unlikely pairing of a Motörhead T-shirt and tan leather jacket, Thomas railed against the probing of pundits Eddie Butler and Jonathan Davies. Writing in his autobiography, Thomas claimed that his parents, up in the producers' gallery at BBC Wales, were witness to then-BBC Wales sport chief Nigel Walker ordering his panel to 'pull out… you look like you're bullying him'.[33]

'It was quite bonkers television,' wrote Ian Gough some years later. 'Alfie always was a player's player. He was a good guy and a good captain, but I would say that, to a man, the squad were sat on their sofas thinking to themselves, "Nooo, this is descending into disaster now." It wasn't just car-crash television; the entire situation had become a complete farce.'[34]

Thomas hadn't been feeling well for a number of weeks, not since being on the end of a ferocious tackle in a recent game for his club Toulouse. After the *Scrum V* debacle, he went home and the ruptured artery in his neck which had resulted from that tackle caused him to have a stroke. He missed the rest of the season.

Scott Johnson – felt by many to be the orchestrator of much of the disharmony – assumed the reins for the remainder of the Six Nations. By the end of the tournament, he had gone too.

Gareth Jenkins was finally appointed to the role that seemed to be made for him. Ron Jones had no doubt that Jenkins deserved the job: 'Gareth is one of those geniuses, an amazing boy, one of the most intelligent I've ever met. Rough at the edges, but bloody hell he's a good boy. One of the most frightening experiences I had was watching a game at the Principality with Gareth, a coincidence, we were sitting next to each other, right at the top. And halfway through I had to say to him, "Gareth mun, shut up, you're ruining the game for me." He was insisting on telling me what was going to happen next. I wouldn't see it, you wouldn't see it, but he'd say, "They're going to do this" – he'd mapped it all out.'[35]

***

Those with fond memories of the Anglo-Welsh tussles of the amateur era were overjoyed at their resurrection, with Welsh teams being invited into the Powergen Cup, making it a 16-team, four-pool tournament. It would commence in the 2005–06 season. The competition, in its early years, was a real throwback to those much-missed days. It was, however, the cause of some angst. Wales' partners in the Celtic League were unimpressed at what they suspected was an attempt by the Welsh regions to find a way out of the Celtic League and into the Guinness Premiership.

'We are totally committed to the Celtic League,' said Llanelli's chairman Stuart Gallacher in response. 'We told Ireland and Scotland today that we would sign a three- or five-year deal guaranteeing our participation on a home-and-away basis. The English have a league which is competitive and financially buoyant, and we will not be joining it.'[36]

The Welsh clubs were briefly ejected from the Celtic League. The agreement which allowed them to return saw them having to give up a significant portion of the £200,000 each of the regions would receive for playing in the Anglo-Welsh Cup.[37] The new tournament would capture the public imagination, with the Scarlets beating Bath at a Millennium Stadium semi-final double-header, before succumbing to Wasps in the inaugural final at Twickenham. The Ospreys followed up by reaching the following season's final, where they were beaten by Leicester.

The national team struggled through the 2006–07 season, drawing a game they should have won against Australia, and again falling to a heavy defeat to the All Blacks. The Six Nations saw Wales back in a familiar position – needing to beat England in the final game to avoid the wooden spoon. They did, and it probably saved Gareth Jenkins' job.

A heartbreaking last-play defeat in the first of the summer Tests in Australia was perhaps surprising, given not only recent performances but also the jetlag-recovery protocol drawn up by the management on arrival.

'These days,' remembered Lee Byrne in his autobiography, 'arriving on southern hemisphere soil would no doubt be followed by an early night and a recovery session the next day. But Gareth had other ideas. "Right boys," he said in the arrivals terminal. "I've had a word with the doctor, and he says the best way to get over the trip is 'jet lag rules.' Ten pints and no spewing."'[38]

While beer legs seemed to carry the team to the verge of a first Test victory, the magic power of jetlag rules presumably wore off, and the second Test was a 31–0 thrashing. But worse was to come. With the Rugby World Cup in France looming, Wales arranged a warm-up game at Twickenham, picked a severely depleted team, and were demolished 62–5. Gareth Jenkins confused onlookers by claiming that England had only managed three line-breaks, despite scoring eight tries.[39]

Wales limped into the Rugby World Cup in France in September 2007, but were dumped out of the pool stages for the third time in five World Cups, this time by Fiji in Nantes.

Up in the stands, Roger Lewis – who had been appointed WRU chief executive in the autumn of 2006 – watched the final moments of Wales' campaign. His reaction to the team's elimination was swift and brutal. He beckoned David Pickering, WRU chairman, towards the pitch. Lewis wanted some privacy to talk, and a body-strewn pitch in the immediate aftermath of a Rugby World Cup match in front of still-rolling cameras appeared to fit the bill.

'I said to David – and the words of Oliver Cromwell at the execution of Charles I echoed in my head: "As a matter of cruel necessity, the coach has to go."'[40]

It was a perhaps unusual thought to have crossed Lewis' mind since, to this day, historians appear to have little to say about Cromwell's approach to rugby administration, while rugby writers rarely find themselves reporting on royal executions.

Back at the team hotel, Jenkins hadn't even negotiated the car park before Lewis and Pickering headed him off and informed him that he had been relieved of his position. The three then walked into the team room, where the crestfallen squad had congregated. Lewis addressed them, as Adam Jones recalls: 'What he was about to do illustrated that beneath his avuncular exterior lay a ruthless businessman. Gareth Jenkins stood alongside him with his head bowed. He'd just been sacked. It was inevitable, but it still felt brutal. Roger explained what had happened in formal, diplomatic language. He said that the two of them had had a frank discussion, and it was felt that Gareth had taken the team as far as he was able to. It was time for someone else to take over.'

Back at the Vale of Glamorgan, Jenkins asked to be let off the team bus so that he could walk the service route, rather than the main route, to the hotel. He didn't want to face the gathered press pack.

'Gareth stood up, with his bag of duty free in one hand – a couple of Toblerones and a bottle of whisky – and he bade us all farewell. No valedictory speech this time. Just a brief thanks, and he was gone. He walked up the lane on his own, wheeling his suitcase and clutching his plastic bag. It was a scene dripping with melancholy. He looked smaller, less commanding, like the whole experience had robbed him of his vitality.'[41]

Ian Gough was perplexed by Jenkins' treatment, but had perhaps spotted something about the character of the new CEO: 'I believe that he deserved to be, and should have been treated with far more dignity than he was at the time. I can only imagine how much he was hurting at the pretty public humiliation he suffered, which seemed designed purely to generate the right newspaper headlines.'[42]

Lewis may have been new on the scene, but he had shown a ruthless streak. His tenure over the following years would push Welsh rugby into a protracted civil war from which it has, arguably, never recovered.

CHAPTER 6

The Most Powerful Man in Rock

'You have to be of a certain age to remember the
moment... when Derek Quinnell... fought his way
through a scrum of stewards and blazers... and burst on
to the field to win his first cap, against France. In case
you are too young to remember, this entrance symbolised
the desire of a Welshman to play for his country; nobody
was going to stand in his way.
'It is a joke currently doing the rounds of the clubs of Wales
that in any race to make it to the pitch on time, Quinnell
the Elder would have been trampled under the feet of
Roger Lewis... It has been officially ratified that our Rog
can go from the posh seats into the arms of the lads quicker
than Justin Tipuric in a Tardis.'[1]

(Eddie Butler on Roger Lewis in 'Wales regions'
chorus of anger finds voice against WRU's Roger Lewis',
The Guardian, 6 April 2013)

ROGER LEWIS HAD taken an unusual route to the top job in
Welsh rugby. Starting out as a musician, he quickly found
himself in a senior role at the BBC: 'I was described as "the
most powerful man in rock music". I hung out with all the
stars, including Madonna who invited me to a big party in

London, Spandau Ballet, Eric Clapton, Tina Turner, Wham! and Bob Geldof, whose house I spent two weeks at.'[2]

Having dispensed with Gareth Jenkins, Lewis acted swiftly as he 'scoured the world' for a new head coach for the national team and alighted on the former Wasps and Ireland coach, Warren Gatland. The New Zealand Rugby Football Union (NZRFU), in Gatland's words, were: 'less than impressed that a Welsh delegation should have flown into the country while a World Cup was in progress on the far side of the equator, but as Roger put it: "My father once told me that if you're going to burgle a house, it's sensible to do it while the occupants are out."'[3]

Wales entered the Gatland era with a cautious sense of optimism. The relationship between the professional teams and the union appeared to be positive, with Lewis announcing that an agreement had been reached in principle on a new operating agreement, gushing: 'We have proved today that the WRU and the regions speak with one voice on wanting to achieve a bright and successful future for our national game. The great thing is that our discussions going forward will be based on trust, respect, and transparency. We will talk straight but talk true.'[4]

With little time to impose his vision on his new charges, Gatland decided to pick 13 Ospreys players to start the first game of the Six Nations. Wales hadn't won at Twickenham for 20 years, and, for 45 minutes, looked destined for the customary biennial thrashing. Trailing 19–6, and hanging on for dear life, something happened. Whether it was a sudden burst of Welsh self-belief, or an uncharacteristic collapse of English self-regard, the tide turned. Wales slowly turned up the pressure, playing carefully and with structure, and their opponents wilted. In an implosion of both cosmic and comic proportions, England at one point managed to throw four consecutive passes, none of which reached their target, losing 50 metres, and ending with a penalty to Wales on the

England 22. From there, Wales scored 20 unanswered points. Scotland and Italy were dispatched in a display of riotous running rugby. The Triple Crown was secured, in Dublin, in a performance of ferocious, relentless discipline which would become a hallmark of the Gatland era. A tight championship decider against France exploded into life on the hour, Wales running in two tries in the final quarter to secure the Grand Slam with a 17-point win.

Domestically, the Ospreys became the first Welsh team to lift the Anglo-Welsh Cup, defeating Leicester, their conquerors of the previous season, in front of over 65,000 supporters at Twickenham. Cardiff Blues finished a close second to Leinster in the Celtic League, although it was a generally poor season for the Welsh teams. In Europe, the Ospreys – having hammered Saracens just two weeks previously in the Anglo-Welsh Cup – succumbed to the same opponents at the quarter-final stage, while Cardiff were handily beaten in Toulouse.

Off the field, two of the regions moved to new homes. A 15,000-seater stadium on the outskirts of Llanelli would be the new home of the Scarlets. Crucially, with a long lease and in partnership with the local authority, the Scarlets had an asset which would prove vital in securing their future. Cardiff, meanwhile, followed the Ospreys route of moving to share a stadium with the city's football club. It was to be an unhappy move for the capital city region.

Grand Slam champions Wales then headed off to South Africa and came down to earth with a bump. Despite some typical sorcery by Shane Williams, and the identification of a novel approach – with erstwhile full-back Jamie Roberts winning his first cap at centre – an injury-weakened Wales lost the Tests by 26 and 16 points respectively.

The slight sense of gloom was further deepened by the realisation that the WRU and regions were not, after all, close to concluding discussions on a new operating agreement.

'It was like the director-general of the CBI leaving to head up the TUC,' wrote Paul Rees in the *Guardian*[5] as – to everybody's amazement – erstwhile WRU group chief executive David Moffett strode back into Welsh rugby, this time as the interim CEO of a new organisation called Regional Rugby Wales. Its purpose was to give the four professional teams a collective voice in their discussions with the WRU.

It didn't go well. Within six months, no agreement had been reached and Moffett had gone again, leaving Llanelli's Stuart Gallacher in charge. The pair blamed the WRU's intransigence for the failure to agree a new deal. Many years later, Moffett trains his sights on the regions: 'Mike Cuddy asked me to go and set up and run Regional Rugby Wales, and I said I'd go and do that. So, I went over there, and I tried. But trying to get the heads of those four teams together was like trying to herd cats. And in the end I got fed up of it, and I jumped on a plane and I said, "Fuck off, I'm not going to do this any longer"… it was a combination of reasons, but what really did it for me was that the four regions couldn't get their acts together, couldn't agree on anything, and I was pushing shit uphill, and I've got better things to do with my time than that. So, I just left them to their own devices.'[6]

Wales missed out on an opportunity to win a second successive Triple Crown for the first time in 30 years – Stephen Jones' last-minute long-range penalty falling just short, handing Ireland a first Grand Slam in 61 years. Those two teams formed the bulk of the touring party to South Africa that summer for one of the great – albeit ultimately unsuccessful – Lions' series.

By October 2009, the WRU and Regional Rugby Wales had signed a new five-year agreement – or, in the WRU's words, 'a new operational roadmap'. A far-reaching agreement, it allowed for the national team to play up to 13 Test matches per season plus up to two non-Test games on annual tours. Players called up by Wales would be released 13 days before the first match of each Test window. Seventeen of the players in each regional match-day squad would have to be Welsh-qualified. Further, the regions would be permitted only six non-Welsh-qualified (NWQ) players, plus two players serving their residency periods, in their wider squads. Regional academies, to this point managed by the union, were devolved to the regions, and they would operate alongside the WRU's national academy. Development regions were agreed in principle, with the first to be established in Colwyn Bay to serve the north of the country. For this, the WRU's direct payments to the regions – as opposed to passported through competition monies – would increase from £3.6m to £6m per year. A new management board would also be created, with both the union and the four regions involved, to monitor the implementation of the new agreement.[7] The agreement would run for five years but could be rolled on at the same terms at the collective discretion of the regions.

It would not be rolled on. It signalled, in fact, the beginning of a significant rebalancing of the delicate relationships in Welsh rugby towards the national team, and it would become the cause of perhaps the greatest schism in the Welsh game in... well, in a few years, at least. But then these kinds of conflagrations tend to come around quite often in Welsh rugby.

The new north Wales region – set up as a cooperative community interest company in 2009, went to the wall barely two years later. The WRU stepped in and ran the development region under the banner of the WRU north Wales academy, as a central concern, and placed it – as a club – into the Welsh premiership.[8]

Two poor Six Nations campaigns in 2010 and 2011 were a cause of concern, but a raft of younger players had been introduced. The regional academies were now churning out players as if they were going out of fashion. The inaugural Under-20 world championship was held in Wales in 2008. The hosts performed creditably, reaching the semi-finals before bowing out to perennial champions New Zealand. Nevertheless, that team-sheet featured players who would become modern greats – Leigh Halfpenny, Jonathan Davies, Dan Biggar, Justin Tipuric and Rhys Webb were among those captained by Sam Warburton. It was some age group.

Some of that crop – notably Halfpenny and Warburton – helped Cardiff Blues to become the first Welsh team to win a European trophy in 2010, beating Toulon in a thriller in Marseille to take the Challenge Cup. In the inaugural Celtic League grand final the following week, the Ospreys defeated Leinster in Dublin.

The class of 2008 was fast-tracked into the senior set-up, supplemented by still young but by now experienced operators such as Jamie Roberts and Alun Wyn Jones, and even younger players such as Taulupe Faletau. They helped inspire a glorious run to the semi-finals of the Rugby World Cup in 2011 – as impossible to imagine earlier that year as it was joyous to behold. An early red card for captain Sam Warburton and – arguably just as importantly – an injury to Adam Jones prevented a first-ever appearance in a Rugby World Cup final. Over 60,000 people gathered at the Millennium Stadium early on an October Sunday morning to watch the game on the big screens. Rugby had recaptured the Welsh imagination.

At least at international level.

By the end of 2011, concerns were being raised at the apparent decline in attendance figures at regional level. The Scarlets were drawing the largest average crowds at a little over 7,200, while the Dragons were bringing up the rear at just 4,766.[9] Yes, the best players had been away at the Rugby World Cup for much of the first half of the season, but the boom in interest in the national team had not translated to the professional teams.

French clubs now identified the crop of talented young Welsh players as ideal transfer targets. James Hook left for Perpignan, Lee Byrne for Clermont Auvergne, Mike Phillips for Bayonne, and Leigh Halfpenny would soon depart for Toulon and Luke Charteris for Racing 92. Nigel Davies, then head coach at the Scarlets and former assistant coach with Wales, claimed that clubs such as Castres – not, by any stretch, the richest or most glamorous in France – were operating with squad budgets three times larger than their Welsh counterparts.[10]

They were further advantaged by French tax laws which allowed a player to ring-fence 30% of his income as image rights, which would not, therefore, be subject to income taxation. Alun Carter and Nick Bishop estimated that, as a result, a salary of £175,000 in France would be worth £250,000 in Wales.[11]

Jamie Roberts recalls Roger Lewis' reaction when they met to discuss the former's potential move to Paris a year later: 'He basically wanted to know how much they were offering to pay me, and when I told him, he just chuckled to himself and brought the meeting to a swift end.'[12]

Running the four regional teams cost a combined £30m. Just £6m reached the teams in direct payments from the WRU – for access to the regions' employees – with another £9m in TV and competition money passported straight through – and finances were stretched. In response, the regions agreed to impose a cap of £3.5m on the salary costs of their first-team squads. English clubs operated on a cap of £4m, which at least meant that the Welsh teams could remain competitive. For the time being.

Financial pressures caused players to leave, and – at the Ospreys – brought about the beginning of the end of the Galacticos era, as Lee Byrne recalled: 'Looking back, I suppose it was the end of a golden era for Ospreys rugby. From 2011, with the region shedding many of its best players amid cost-cutting measures, the club was no longer able to compete consistently on the biggest stage (although they did brilliantly to win the league again in 2012). As a group of players and coaches, we had much to be proud of. Yes, we'd come up short in Europe. But with an Anglo-Welsh trophy win and now two league titles in four seasons, we'd proved ourselves to be one of the best teams in Britain.'[13]

The financial struggles at regional level were difficult to understand, given the burgeoning bank balance of the WRU. By 2012, Roger Lewis was boasting that he had overseen a 44% increase in turnover to £63m and a 31% increase in earnings in his five years in charge. Where was that money going?

Perhaps it was all being spent on the national team which, after all, had just chalked up a second Grand Slam of the Gatland era, and a third in seven years? That achievement alone – although the overall record of the modern vintage was much more variable – echoed that of the great teams of the 1970s. The summer tour to Australia saw three narrow, heartbreaking defeats but, at Test level, things hadn't been quite this good for a long time.

The WRU and the regions jointly announced that they would commission PricewaterhouseCoopers to undertake a financial review of the professional game. PwC's findings, when they reported in late 2012, were alarming.

The regions, they reported, were not sustainable businesses in their current form without substantial additional funding from benefactors. The funding gap – the gap between spending and income – had increased from £2m in 2008 to £5.2m in 2011 despite a £5m increase in revenue over that period. Poor business planning by the regions was partly to blame. Benefactors had continued to meet these shortfalls, but the report noted that 'benefactors becoming disillusioned with a relationship of conflict has removed most or all of this support for the regional businesses'. The regions' collective action in instituting a salary cap would, PwC felt, remove the funding gap in its entirety by 2013. Yet again, the view was that the WRU and regions needed to work more closely together. However, the report concluded that greater central control – whether in treating the regions as WRU subsidiary companies or taking on greater responsibility for central contracting – would not be welcomed by the WRU.[14]

However, Roger Lewis saw things differently.

'My ideal model would be complete WRU ownership of the four teams with sufficient devolved responsibility to enable them to go about their businesses as they see fit. But that's not what we're looking at here. What we're working on is a hybrid – a system of joint control.'

Lewis not only diverged from the PwC report. He also seemed to diverge from the general view of the state of his relationship with the regions: 'The meetings we're presently engaged in are between like-minded people; realistic, logical men; good men; people who are leaders in both business and rugby and are happy to play their part in honest, objective discussions about where we go from here. In this sense, our relationship with the regions is better than it's ever been. There is no red mist, there are no cheap shots. These are fruitful talks and I feel very positive that a sensible agreement can be reached.'

Lewis had, of course, expressed very similar sentiments three years previously. Just before the regions formed Regional Rugby Wales, brought David Moffett back from New Zealand to fight their corner, and had threatened to withhold their players from the national team.

Ominously, and in a portent of what was to come in the following years, Lewis had words of warning for the regions: 'Look, if any of the four regions wanted to pay off their debts and sort out their loans, I'd be happy to take the keys off them. What I won't do is take on their liabilities.'[15]

A significant proportion of the union's finances were being directed at paying off the stadium debt. David Moffett couldn't understand this approach at all: 'In chasing the debt repayment, they are keeping the game poor, not only at professional level but also at club level. It just doesn't make any sense to keep the game poor just so that you can say, "Well, we'll be debt-free by 2020" or whatever it is.'[16]

Indeed, it was understood that, by 2012, the union's repayment of its stadium debt was approximately 30 years ahead of schedule.

Among the key findings of the PwC report was that there should be greater collaboration between the union and the regions. A working group of sorts had been in place to review playing aspects of the agreement signed by all parties in 2009, but it now needed to be empowered to consider financial issues too. The Professional Regional Game Board (PRGB) was formed just before Christmas 2012. It would include one representative of each of the four regions, four representatives of the Welsh Rugby Union, and an independent chair.

For the first time in a while, the national team appeared to be struggling. Warren Gatland had been awarded a season-long sabbatical from his highly-paid job as Wales' head coach to prepare for the following summer's Lions tour to Australia, which he would lead. Wales lost all four autumn internationals under caretaker head coach Robert Howley which, together with the three defeats in Australia in the summer, saw the national team fall outside the top eight on the IRB world rankings. The effect was serious. Wales – semi-finalists at the World Cup 13 months earlier, and Grand Slam champions – would be among the third group of seeds in the draw for the next tournament.

Back in domestic rugby, things in the PRGB garden weren't so much not-that-rosy as it's-all-weeds-and-even-the-weeds-are-on-fire bad, complete with calls for independent arbitration.

A letter sent to all member clubs by Roger Lewis in February 2013 claimed that the regions wanted control of the whole game in Wales. RRW shot back that they wanted to 'deal in facts and cannot also just sit by and watch the Welsh rugby public subjected to misleading spin'.[17]

Wales recovered from an eighth successive loss – to Ireland in the first game of the 2013 Six Nations – with a second successive title, thumping England by a record 27-point margin in the final game.

Yet barely two weeks later, the heat in the simmering civil war between the regions and the union was turned up a notch.

The Scarlets – having unearthed a large pool of young top-class players who, in negotiating their second professional contracts, they found they could no longer afford – had reached an agreement with Northampton. George North, at that time possibly the most exciting winger in the world game, would move to the English club at the end of the season. The transfer fee would allow the Scarlets to reinvest. The WRU were far from happy. They claimed to have offered to centrally contract North, but that RRW's policy of not fielding centrally contracted players prohibited such a move. They accused the Scarlets of touting North to the highest bidder in England and France.[18]

RRW, collectively, responded: 'The four Welsh regions are united in expressing how staggered and bitterly disappointed they all are with the nature, intent and content of the public statement made by the WRU this morning on a number of issues affecting Welsh rugby.'[19]

By the autumn, the future of European tournaments was in doubt. English and French clubs had given notice two years earlier that they would quit the existing competitions by the beginning of the 2014–15 season. High up their list of grievances was the split of revenues – of the £44m generated by the Heineken Cup the previous season in sponsorship and broadcasting deals, 52% went to Celtic League countries. The French and the English wanted an equal three-way split between the three leagues. Welsh regions – pushed into a corner by the collapse of the relationship with the WRU – backed the Anglo-French proposal, seeing a way of achieving ownership of a portion of any new competition. In the meantime, the existing framework agreement between the WRU and the regions – signed in 2009 – would expire in the summer of 2014. The WRU set a deadline of 31 December 2013 for the conclusion of negotiations on a new deal, emphasising that they saw it as a simple matter of rolling on the existing agreement for another five years. The union often claimed that payments were, in fact, in the region of £16m. However, over £9m came directly from broadcasting and participation payments to competing teams in the RaboDirect Pro12 (Celtic) League and Heineken Cup – money which was owed directly to the clubs by the organisers, and which was merely passported through the union's accounts.

At the time, the real WRU payment to the regions amounted to £6.6m per year. Of that, £2.4m was split four ways as core grant, a further £2.4m was split four ways as a limit for non-Welsh-qualified players, £0.6m contributed towards the four regional academies, with the remaining £1.2m as compensation for releasing Wales players for extra training and extra matches not sanctioned specifically by the IRB Test window. By means of comparison, the RFU in England paid its clubs £13.75m in compensation for the additional release of players alone.[20]

The regions demurred.

The scene was set for a tumultuous 18 months which would push Welsh rugby close to the precipice.

CHAPTER 7

One for You, Two for Me

'The four regions and the Welsh Rugby Union agreed…
that if one doesn't sign an agreement, well there is no
region, and that is the consequence of not signing an
agreement… they would not be playing in Europe, they
would not be playing in Rabo, they'd not be receiving the
monies off the Welsh Rugby Union, they would not have
insurance off the Welsh Rugby Union for their players
and they would not have any referees.'[1]

(Roger Lewis, speaking to BBC Wales
Scrum V, October 2013)

THE STAND-OFF OVER Europe meant that the regions were
unwilling to sign a new agreement with the WRU, stating,
understandably, that they needed certainty over the
competitions in which they would be playing. A corollary of
the impasse was that the regions were unable to offer new
contracts to those whose agreements ran out at the end of the
season.

Alun Wyn Jones, Sam Warburton, Adam Jones, Jonathan
Davies, and Ian Evans were among those affected. The
WRU, having set aside £1m to help with the retention of key
players, offered to sign leading players on central contracts,
undertaking to transfer those contracts – on the completion of
discussions around the competition structure for the following
season – back to the regions.

Regional Rugby Wales had agreed that they would, collectively, refuse to play any centrally contracted players. Lewis insisted that he was working in the best interests of Welsh rugby as a whole. The whole did not seem to include supporters of the professional teams. They had been largely ignored, despite their money being crucial in supporting the infrastructure of elite rugby. Supporters' groups and trusts were quickly formed. Barrie Jones, a long-term member of the Scarlets' supporters' trust, Crys 16, felt that he had to get involved: 'Throughout the stand-alone campaign, I did very little in terms of hands-on activity. Yes, I complained from the sidelines. It was in the early days of social media so I did more than my fair share of online moaning. Consequently, I vowed never to be so passive again. I was present at the first-ever meeting to discuss the formation of a supporters' trust in February 2006. I am still involved.'[2]

The various groups and trusts came together to form the Joint Supporters Group (JSG). Their intention was to strengthen their collective voice. When they threatened to stage protests at the Christmas 2013 derbies, in part because the WRU had refused repeated requests to meet with a delegation of fans, they quickly found that they had the ear of both the professional teams and the WRU. Within days, the WRU had agreed to meet. At that meeting, Lewis reiterated that the five-year agreement signed in 2009 was, in effect, a ten-year agreement. Suggestions that the WRU had advised key out-of-contract players not to sign with their regions were rejected by Warren Gatland.[3]

However, increasing doubt was being cast about Roger Lewis' often-repeated assertion that he would always act openly and transparently.

'Not one of life's natural Trappists,'[4] his thirst for the limelight had become a subject of some comment.

Yet he appeared strangely reluctant to take responsibility for elements of his record which were not universally applauded. Having told the *Independent*'s Chris Hewett in 2012 that he had 'personally negotiated a television deal for them [the regions] in respect of the Celtic League, or the RaboDirect Pro12 as it is now. Together with the money from European tournaments – and I've spent six years on the European Rugby Cup board ensuring income is maximised – that realises £9m a year,' he later told the JSG that TV deals were nothing to do with him. In fact, they were negotiated collectively by Celtic League Ltd and ERC Ltd, of which – he was keen to stress – the regions were a part.[5]

'He is safe for the moment,' wrote Eddie Butler, 'because in photos, where he stands beaming among the lads, having rushed down from above, you cannot hear the jeers of the people.'[6]

The JSG then had an opportunity to meet with Regional Rugby Wales. The previous week's meeting with the WRU formed the basis of the agenda, with each of the union's assertions challenged in turn. Most notably, Roger Lewis' statement that existing contractual agreements prevented any possibility of restructuring European competition, nor of exploring potential partnerships with English clubs, was dismissed. On the contrary, said RRW's Stuart Gallacher, the only existing contractual commitments were the existing partnership agreement and the ERC (European Rugby Cup) accord, both of which would expire at the end of the season. The Celtic accord, which obliged the WRU to enter teams into the Celtic (by now RaboDirect) League, did not involve the existing regions – the WRU was the sole Welsh signatory.[7]

Indeed, and directly contradicting Lewis' denials, RRW provided evidence to the JSG that he had been invited to meetings to discuss a potential Anglo-Welsh partnership. Lewis' further claim that he had, in fact, proactively proposed an Anglo-Welsh League to English clubs, and that they had rejected the notion, was roundly rebuffed – it had not been a proposal, said Gallacher, more a throwaway comment over lunch.

The financial costs of playing in the RaboDirect Pro12 League were stark. Flights to away games came in at £1m across the four professional teams. Given the geographic location of teams within the league, very few away fans attended games in Wales, affecting attendances (although the two western regions, in the 2013 season, were exceeding the 8,000 average attendances which had been set as a target on their formation in 2003, while Cardiff Blues were only 200 short). Steps which had been taken to increase payments to the regions had been loaded in the union's favour. Key among these was the fourth autumn international which, the union had claimed, had been agreed mainly to increase the budget available to the regions. RRW stated that the income from the game amounted to over £2.5m. Australia, the first opponents in the additional, out-of-window fixture, had been paid £750,000 to play. The regions had received £100,000 each. The union – admittedly with the costs of staging the matches to bear – took the rest. And the additional fixture ate into the regions' preparation time for the pre-Christmas block of European matches.

With no prospect of resolution by the union's self-imposed deadline of 31 December, the supporters took their protest to the festive derbies. Banners urging all parties to 'Protect Our Game' were flown to the acclaim of those present.

English clubs were in a battle of their own. Having long given notice that they would – along with their French counterparts – quit the existing European tournaments at the end of the season, and with the union-led nations refusing to countenance their demands for greater control, they were keenly aware of the gaps in their fixture lists. Before the new year, news broke of an offer made to the Welsh regions to join the English premiership from the start of the 2014–15 season. Each region would receive £4m per season, and there would be a guarantee that at least three of the four regions would play in the top-flight at any one time.[8]

The regions argued that they had no choice but to explore a tie-in with English clubs: 'In addition to being unable to confirm the structure of their European competition, the WRU is unable to fully confirm the number of teams competing in the Pro12 between 14/15 and 18/19, the revenue from and distribution from the league in that period. There is currently no sponsor for the Pro12 in 2014/15 and the TV deals are not confirmed. We don't even know what will happen in six months' time when the current PA expires. This is despite the WRU knowing of the uncertainty around European competition for almost two years, and the Pro12 for approaching one year. The regions have been put in a position where their entire business platform in just six months' time is completely unknown, with a combined revenue risk of £16m, yet they are being pressurised by the WRU to sign a five-year extension to the PA immediately!'

It was widely understood that the Anglo-Welsh proposal would proceed only if no European competition could be agreed for the following season.

The union retaliated with rumoured plans to establish three new regions in Neath, Pontypridd, and a location in north Wales. They would look to centrally contract key players.[9]

'We have an opportunity to play in a lucrative new Cup competition, while staying within the WRU and remaining in the Pro12,' said Peter Thomas. 'If we can't do that with the support and blessing of our governing body, then we will have to look at alternative options... Plan A is the Rugby Champions Cup. But people would be foolish to think there is not a Plan B. We need to play in a meaningful, financially viable competition.'[10]

The major obstacle to an agreement between the union and regions was, in the eyes of the regions, and as explained by Peter Thomas – Roger Lewis: 'There is desire within the WRU but there is no appetite for the regions to work with Roger Lewis. We have no confidence in him. His agenda is to destroy the regions and take complete control.'

A further source claimed that the union's intention to centrally contract players was even more convoluted than it had first appeared. They would be contracted to the union, and then loaned to English clubs.[11]

It had previously been alleged that the WRU were, in fact, attempting to coerce players into signing central contacts rather than re-signing with their present regions. The WRU denied the charge to the JSG in December, but Alastair Eykyn on the BBC reported that: 'I have it on very good authority that Alun Wyn Jones is being harassed almost daily by those at the WRU, from Roger Lewis and Warren Gatland, to sign a central contract so that they can maintain control of him... What they want is one big signing now, big splash across all the newspapers, lots of momentum behind them, and then, suddenly, everything begins to fall into place.'[12]

And then, with matters fraught enough, David Moffett reappeared. Again.

'I was watching things from afar, and people were telling me things, and I got so fed up with watching on at what was going on with Lewis, that I decided that I would go over there. My intention was to get rid of Lewis and Pickering.'[13]

The BBC's *Scrum V* programme held a *Question Time*-style panel show on 19 January 2014. Among the panellists were the Dragons' Gareth Davies, journalist Paul Rees and, an arrival shortly before the recording started, Roger Lewis.

Sold as an opportunity to question the panellists, audience members had prepared their comments. Gwladrugby's Dan Allsobrook was in the audience on that January Sunday morning and saw something very different: 'It quickly became clear that we were just there as padding and spent most of the morning listening to the panel discussing pre-agreed topics with a handful of opinions from selected audience members rather than questions. There were no opportunities to put any questions forward to the panel once the cameras started rolling. The production team had specifically asked us to provide questions prior to the recording. None of our questions were used.

'Our frustration turned to anger when we watched the recording later that day. We had not expected much having been there, but at the very least we thought we'd had a chance to react to what the panellists were saying. None of this was reflected in the edition which went to air.

'Several of the comments made by Roger Lewis were followed by jeering and various comments were clearly audible from the audience. However, the audience reaction only came across once during the broadcast version of the show, which made the debate seem much more amicable and considerably less confrontational than it was. Even some of the more confrontational comments from the panel and host were edited out, for example when [*Scrum V* host] Gareth Lewis pushed Roger Lewis for an answer as to whether the WRU had looked to set up new regions.

'There were several further examples of this, with what appeared to be the one common theme: the show was edited in order to be favourable to the WRU and Roger Lewis. For those of us in the studio, there was no question that there was a very clear discontent with the WRU from the majority of the audience which did not come across in the final edit.

'A few weeks later an article was published by the WalesEye website which carried claims from a "BBC programme maker" claiming that Paul Rees was "effectively gagged" and removed from a subsequent programme's panel because "senior management decided his views on the Welsh Rugby Union were 'inappropriate'".

'Rees was asked, by a researcher for the programme, to outline some of the key points he would make. He was, of course, a member of the panel at the *Scrum V* debate in

January and stated that he would maintain his critical tone. It is alleged that the matter of his participation on the programme was "referred up" to senior figures, after which it was decided to "stand him down" from contributing to the programme. WalesEye's source, a BBC Wales programme-maker, was quoted saying that: "It's disheartening when you are trying to make a programme that reflects all sides in a debate, to be told that certain things just cannot be said.'"[14]

A letter of complaint was sent by Allsobrook and others to the BBC. Their concerns were rejected.

Having appeared on the *Scrum V* show, Roger Lewis was keen to emphasise that he wished to keep discussions behind closed doors.

'With respect, we have not been playing this out in the public domain. The Welsh Rugby Union has kept its counsel, we've retained our dignity and only now this week are we discussing these matters with yourselves. We've not been issuing press releases. We've not been going to the press discussing these matters. We have always wanted to have our negotiations behind closed doors but we are where we are, and we now have to look to the future.'

In fact, Lewis claimed that 'in the world's view, they're slightly bemused because Welsh rugby is in such a strong place as far as world rugby is concerned'.[15]

He made those comments on ITV, following up on a leaked letter to the WRU's member clubs in which he criticised the regions' flawed business model, and various media appearances in which he announced that the WRU had set aside £1m to directly contract some players, talked about the obstacles delaying the resolution of outstanding issues, that the regions could cease to exist, and criticising the Scarlets for their handling of the George North transfer to Northampton.[16]

Wales captain Sam Warburton became the first – and only – player to sign a central contract with the WRU. The agreement meant that the WRU intended to lease him back to Cardiff Blues who, for their part, emphasised that they had agreed through RRW that they would not play centrally contracted players.

European Rugby Cup now failed to make a scheduled payment to the regions worth £800,000. The WRU's response to the late payment highlighted the 'cakeism' of the regime. ERC money was to be paid to participating clubs. It was therefore the property of the regions. However, it passed through the WRU's accounts. So, when payments were made, they were treated as the WRU's income to be paid out to the regions, but when payments were missed, it became the regions' problem.

Robert Davies, a director at the Ospreys, was furious, telling BBC Radio Wales that, even though WRU financial director Steve Phillips had been present at the ERC meeting at which the decision not to make the payment had been taken, he had neglected to tell the regions. They, in turn, had to make their own arrangements to pay their players. He went on: 'I was quite shocked to read your report, the BBC that is, about what Mr Lewis had said and he was saying that, firstly the regions are open to the idea of expanding national contracts – that's untrue. Both sides plan to make more deals – that's untrue. We have a plan on the table that we are discussing – that's untrue. The regions have engaged with that plan – that's untrue. The WRU has been working on the plan for several months – that's untrue. And the regions originally contacted the union to keep six players in Wales – well that's untrue.'

Davies called for the WRU board to step in and to control its executive: 'The union board itself should be looking at itself. I don't think that anybody comes out very well out of this, but the union board itself should have shown more leadership, more decisiveness, more honesty, more integrity. Everybody's complicit in this and we need really to have a look at the way we run the game in Wales.'[17]

RRW followed up with a letter to the chair of the National Assembly's Communities, Equality and Local Government Committee which highlighted its concerns over a lack of trust with the WRU.

'The lack of trust between the WRU... and the regional organisations is at the core of the current dispute about the participation agreement.'[18]

David Moffett now stated his intention to stand for election to the WRU board, although he later admitted that: 'I never had any intention of standing as the chairman, but I thought I'd just throw that in so that I got some media.'[19]

As part of his campaign, Moffett published the 'Moffesto' – a manifesto titled 'One Wales – building a sustainable future together' – in March 2014. The detailed document – launched at the same Castle Hotel in Neath at which the WRU was formed in 1881 – contained a raft of proposals, including ideas around restructuring existing WRU districts into five regional boards which would have a great deal of autonomy, spending on community rugby infrastructure, new and appropriate competition structures at all levels, formal five-year franchises for professional teams, central contracting of professional players, and governance reform.[20]

By April, the risk of a breakaway by the Welsh regions subsided as an agreement was reached for a new European Rugby Champions' Cup – the unions were signatories, along with the professional teams in France, England, and Wales. The regions had secured a stake in the European Cup. Existing broadcasters Sky, and new broadcasters BT, would share coverage of the new tournament.

Dissatisfaction among community clubs about changes to their league structure were seized on by Moffett. He collected the signatures of 43 member clubs, including all four regions, and an emergency general meeting was duly called for 15 June 2014. There were two main resolutions on the agenda. The first stated that the WRU's board of directors had not been acting in the best interests of Welsh rugby. The second was a vote of no confidence in the current board.

Days before the EGM, Moffett closed his Twitter account and announced that he was returning to New Zealand. 'I told everybody that I was going home to New Zealand, but I turned up at the meeting, and I got up to speak, and it was "We don't need you Moffett to tell us what to do", so, you know, it was a bit of a shambles of a meeting.'

Moffett tried to land some early blows, demanding answers from the WRU CEO and chairman about the finances of the union. 'The biggest disaster ever to befall world rugby was that guy [Lewis]. This was the guy that paid back the bank early because he was awash, the union was awash, with cash. He said at that EGM that I forced in 2014 that he didn't understand numbers. So, he caused a lot of trouble.'[21]

But, as in 2002, clubs turned up with their own agenda items.

One representative stood up to complain about being dragged to Port Talbot on a Sunday morning – 'It's Father's Day and my salad's in the oven – can we move on please?'[22]

When he tried to turn the discussion to the WRU's Welsh-language strategy, Moffett received a comprehensive answer, partly in Welsh, from Roger Lewis about a soon-to-be launched new and bilingual WRU website. Moffett, for reasons which have never quite been made clear, answered in Swahili.

He then 'sniffed the breeze', concluded that neither motion would be carried, and suggested abandoning his remaining points. The WRU pressed ahead with a vote regardless.

The vote of no confidence was seen off, with only four votes in favour, 18 abstentions and 462 votes against. The vote on a statement that the WRU had not been acting in the best interests of Welsh rugby was defeated by a similar margin.

Gerald Davies, who had seen all of this before as a member of the Tasker Watkins working party, stood up to close the meeting. His comments should have given Lewis and Pickering pause for thought: 'Our reputation is tarnished and it's not a good image. We are not held in high regard; we are held in low esteem. It is disappointing and distressing we have such a reputation. We need desperately to restore our dignity and reputation. We need a strong identity, we need cohesion, collaboration, and cooperation. We need to restore Welsh rugby and not through self-interest. We can't carry on with having more of the same. We need a right rugby governance Welsh rugby can be proud of. We can't come back here in five years' time for another EGM. If we do, we have failed.'[23]

Gerald had had enough. Shortly after the EGM, he announced that he would not stand again as a national representative and would therefore leave the WRU board.

Within two weeks, the existing partnership agreement between the regions and the WRU expired. Yet again, Roger Lewis claimed that the two parties were close to an agreement. And, yet again, RRW had to correct him. A new draft agreement, prepared by the WRU, was said to be 'completely unacceptable'.

'Sadly', said the regions in a press release in July, 'the regions regret to confirm that despite an indescribably tortuous process of endless telephone calls and meetings since January 6th, the control, commercial and financial conditions that are being demanded of them under drafts of the proposed new service agreement would be completely unacceptable for any responsible independent business to enter into and expose itself to.'

A summary of the RRW statement on ESPN Rugby was damning of the role of the WRU chief executive: 'It is interesting that board members are accused of saying one thing in public but doing another behind closed doors. It seems he remains a major obstacle to any successful resolution. One of the major stumbling blocks is Roger

Lewis, the WRU's far-from-popular chief executive. As he is unlikely to go anywhere, it is a barrier than must be worked around.'[24]

At last, on 28 August, a new five-year, £60m rugby services agreement was signed off. The regions had secured an increase in WRU payments from £6.7m to £8.7m, which included £2m set aside for new dual contracts by the WRU, with a further £1.3m identified by the regions in a 60/40 split which, it was thought, would reflect the amount of time a regular Wales squad player would spend with both his teams. A one-off additional payment of £500,000 per region would be made by the WRU. A senior player selection policy – colloquially known as 'Gatland's Law' – would be instituted, which would prohibit players playing outside Wales from being considered for selection for the national team (although any number of caveats could be applied by national head coach Warren Gatland).

Pickering and Lewis would not be thanked. Ahead of September's annual general meeting, Pickering stood for another term as a national representative and was defeated by Gareth Davies – by now the Newport Gwent Dragons CEO – and Anthony Buchanan. It was a shock, to some.

'The coating of Teflon is starting to melt away from the top echelons of Welsh rugby. The charade played out in the Welsh media that the ruling parties could do no wrong came to an abrupt end last week with the deselection of chairman David Pickering from the board of the Welsh Rugby Union,' wrote former Wales fly-half Paul Turner.[25]

Perhaps the clubs of Wales had grown weary of the disconnect between the way Lewis and Pickering viewed themselves, and the way the rest of Welsh rugby saw them. Pickering, after all, had responded to Gerald Davies' criticisms of the union's hierarchy, and his comments that the union was held in low esteem, with the following: 'The Welsh Rugby Union is held in great esteem in the countries of power within the game for both its governance and the success of its administration.'[26]

Pickering managed, as his final act, to push through some governance changes. A commission, led by Sir Robert Owen, had worked for two years to fashion amendments which would see the creation of two independent non-executive director posts (one of whom, 'ideally', should be a woman) and term limits on members of the WRU board which would prevent members from serving for more than twelve years (although these would not apply retrospectively, and would therefore not affect the half a dozen or so who had survived in situ since the previous millennium).

***

One of the most striking features of the Test team's record during Gatland's period – despite the Grand Slams and championships and contributions to Lions successes – had been its complete lack of success against the three major southern hemisphere nations. The autumn 2014 victory over the South Africans was a first for Wales in 16 encounters with the Springboks since 1999, and only a second win in 27 attempts for Gatland's Wales over one of the big three.

Having secured election to the WRU board, Gareth Davies was persuaded to stand – successfully – for the position of WRU chairman. He was not impressed with what he found: 'When I was made chairman, it was made clear to me – by people in the professional game and the community game – that the chief executive was an issue. It wasn't just confined to Wales either – there were members of other unions who thought the same. After a few months in the role, it was obvious that we were just incompatible – we saw things too differently. So, discussions started with the board, and by early 2015 we'd agreed that Roger would leave the business that year.'[27]

An agreement was eventually reached that Lewis would

stay on until the end of the 2015 Rugby World Cup. His last months saw a flurry of activity, including agreement on a nine-year £33m deal with kit suppliers Under Armour and a ten-year, £13m deal with the Principality Building Society for the naming rights of the Millennium Stadium.

The process of negotiating these deals led to his early release, as Gareth Davies narrates: 'Around the summer of 2015, we were negotiating a number of deals with commercial partners. We had agreed that Roger would stay until the end of the Rugby World Cup, But Roger and I hadn't been seeing eye-to-eye for a while, and it became clear that there were elements of these negotiations with partners which weren't being conducted as I would have liked. We had to have another discussion and we agreed that he would step away a little earlier than planned, and that Martyn Phillips would step up.'[28]

An extraordinary hagiography appeared in the *Western Mail* in October 2015 – written in such glowing terms that it might as well have been crafted by Lewis himself – celebrating a tenure which it presented as an overwhelmingly successful one. Dismissing various criticisms as 'nonsense' and 'social media myth', it painted a uniformly glowing picture of an unprecedentedly turbulent time in Welsh rugby.

No matter. As the then Pontypool RFC CEO Ben Jeffreys wrote: 'Fast-forward to today, and we all know the reality. David Pickering is no longer the chairman and Roger Lewis is no longer the chief executive officer of the WRU. Ultimately, the power evaporated, and influential members of the Welsh rugby public made their message abundantly clear: change was and still is needed.'[29]

After years of rancour, it was hoped that the new era would bring greater cooperation and a sense of common purpose.

CHAPTER 8

Partnership, Reset

'It helps [that the WRU] now wants the regions to succeed
and is trying to make that happen. The wasted years mean
they are still sailing against the current but at least now
there is not a fight for the tiller.'[1]

(Paul Rees in the *Guardian* on the morning of the Scarlets'
Champions' Cup semi-final in Dublin, 2018)

THE WRU WERE back in listening mode. Meetings with the
Joint Supporters Group, abandoned in December 2013, finally
reconvened in April 2015. Newly-installed WRU chairman
Gareth Davies welcomed supporters to the meeting, stating
unequivocally that the WRU was now in a very different place
to 2013, and that he looked forward to the WRU, Professional
Rugby Wales (the newly-rebranded RRW) and the JSG
working together, and not as adversaries.

Wales performed creditably at Rugby World Cup 2015.
Ostensibly an England-hosted event, some matches had been
nabbed for Wales in Cardiff, where they would face Uruguay
and Fiji. The decision to allow head coach Warren Gatland
to take a sabbatical for the entirety of the 2012–13 season
to prepare for the 2013 Lions tour had backfired for Wales
– seven consecutive defeats meant that, when the draw for
RWC 2015 was made, Wales were drawn with Australia and
hosts England and would play both at Twickenham.

A heroic victory over England in their second match meant that England became the first host country to fail to make it out of the pool stages. A frustrating defeat against Australia – where the limitations of Wales' approach were exposed in their repeated failure to break down the, at times, 13-man Wallabies – struck a chord with Lee Byrne, by now out of the squad.

'I suppose an inability to come up with a Plan B is a problem for Welsh teams, including the national side. When I was involved, Gatland would be forever telling us that we were fitter and stronger than the opposition. "Keep going and you'll break them down," he'd say. And obviously we've had success with that approach... But, in the end, teams work out what you're trying to do, so the challenge becomes how to develop your game. With the Wales team, I sometimes felt like we had 100 calls but no idea about where to go when the game plan wasn't working.'[2]

The defeat meant that Wales would face South Africa rather than Scotland in the quarter-finals. Injury-ravaged, they succumbed by four points. Sam Warburton would later say that defeat may have been a blessing – Wales were so weakened by injury that the semi-final against one of the greatest of All Black teams could well have been ugly.

Back in domestic rugby, the regions were struggling. The Scarlets lost all six matches in the pool stages of the European Cup. The Ospreys performed better, but their three victories left them in a three-way tie with Exeter and Bordeaux Bègles, and they were eliminated on tries scored. In the Pro12, the Scarlets were the best of the Welsh teams, finishing fifth, as no Welsh team made the end-of-season play-offs for the first time. With only the top six qualifying for the elite tier of European rugby, Wales would be represented by just one team for the first time in the competition's history the following season. It would also be the first time that the Ospreys, for so long Wales' standard-bearers in Europe in the regional era, would not be at the top table.

At the end of what Shane Williams referred to as 'the worst season in the history of Welsh regional rugby',[3] Gareth Davies announced a review of the performance of the regions.

'It's not crisis time at all, it's time for some level heads. [We must] review what's good and what's not so good... [to] robustly review what happened, where the weaknesses are, where the shortfalls are and how we can start to review [and] repair what has happened this year.'

In a marked departure from what had gone before, Davies added: 'It's a collective responsibility I think, yes, the union has to provide some leadership in all of this and we're trying to do that. We've sat down with colleagues in the regions over the past couple of weeks, not just looking at how we performed this year, but have we got the right people, the right talent in all the positions.'[4]

By the autumn, the WRU had released a new 'Strategy for Welsh Rugby' with the strapline 'more people, more often with more enjoyment and more success'. Newly-appointed WRU chief executive officer Martyn Phillips, recognising the task ahead, said – 'The strategy is the easy bit, our challenge now is to implement, and we cannot do that without the help of the good people volunteering, playing, coaching, refereeing and administrating at rugby clubs the length and breadth of the country' – and set out key strategic outcomes. These would aim to secure the best players and coaches in a high-performance environment, achieve success in the best competitions, attract more supporters more often, secure higher value sponsorship and investment, attract, grow, and retain potential talent as players, coaches and on committees, and reinvest in the game.

Underpinning the vision were more record financial figures – turnover was up by over £10m to £73.3m. More importantly, investment in the game at all levels had increased by double-digit percentages.[5]

The new strategy was broadly welcomed. While necessarily couched in broad terms, there appeared to be an ambition to address many of the issues which had plagued Welsh rugby for decades. A long-term approach would be taken to the planning of the game at all levels, eschewing short-term gain. The language of the strategy suggested moving away from the top-heavy, Team Wales-centric approach of the previous decade. Steps would be taken to remove barriers to participation for women and girls. Engagement and transparency would be watchwords. Yet another review of governance would be undertaken to encourage diversity on boards and committees at all levels.

On the eve of the opening weekend of the 2015 Six Nations, the new administration was struck by the need to drag the WRU into the modern age. Dignitaries and their partners were given their instructions for the weekend's festivities. The men were to be taken by bus to a function at the Celtic Manor hotel. Later, another bus would be sent for their partners, who would also dine at the Celtic Manor, but in a different room. At the match, partners were permitted to attend, but sat behind their menfolk. The administration circulated a note to the board explaining that this practice could not continue.

'I was astounded to see such old-fashioned opinions. We had a discussion with the board to try to persuade them, arguing "Come on guys, it's 2015", that the idea of having separate men's and women's dinners was stupid and that we needed to change it. So, we sought the views of people within the union, and there was still opposition. People would say that it was useful to have men meeting together, and that it was a chance to have sessions of information gathering with their Scottish and English friends and so on. We managed to persuade them of the way forward in the end. But what really frustrated me was that we had a new CEO in place who wanted the board to contribute to the union's new strategy and the governance reforms we were proposing, but some of the board seemed more interested in the formalities around Six Nations games.'[6]

Peter Thomas, at the Cardiff Blues, was hopeful that a new spirit of partnership was in the air: 'It's a breath of fresh air that we've got an executive in Gareth and Martyn who know the game and understand our difficulties. We have a situation where we can sit down and trust one another and that has been a huge step forward. Gareth was my first CEO here and he was also CEO at the Dragons, so he has a great advantage of understanding. What I like about the new executive is they listen.'

Yet he warned that the regions were being left behind by their continental competitors: 'We all realise we cannot compete in either the Pro12 or Europe when we are working on squad costs of £4m to £5m while the Irish and the Scots are at £6.5m to £7m and the English clubs are up at £8m. In fairness to the Welsh Rugby Union, they understand this.'[7]

Among the potential solutions under consideration in early 2017 was a plan to contract all professional players to a new central body made up of the WRU and the regions. Closer to, but not directly copying, the systems operating in New Zealand and Ireland, it would see the pooling of all income into one pot from which all players would be paid. Joint ventures on issues including insurance, medical and office supplies had already been in place for a year or so and had saved around £1m. The new proposal would see all players – not just the 16 or so who were at that point on national dual contracts (NDCs) – paid from a central pot which, crucially, would maintain the independence of the four regions.[8]

For the first time in five years, a Welsh team reached the final of the Pro12 in 2016–17. The Scarlets had put together a run of form in the latter half of the season built on their own academy pipeline with the addition of a handful of quality, but under-appreciated, players from elsewhere. The likes of McNicholl, Beirne, Barclay and Parkes, supplemented by returning Test players, needed only 14 men to see off Leinster in Dublin, before returning to the city two weeks later to demolish Munster in a riotous, scarcely believable display of running rugby.

Warren Gatland had been away for most of the season on another sabbatical as he prepared to lead the Lions to New Zealand. It didn't work for Wales, whose two victories under interim head coach Robert Howley left them in fifth place, their worst Six Nations placing in a decade. It worked for the Lions, however, who avoided defeat in a series in New Zealand for the first time since 1971.

The summer and early autumn of 2017 brought a reality check.

In May, the Newport Gwent Dragons – 50% owned by the WRU since Ebbw Vale's withdrawal in 2003 – became an entirely WRU-run entity. The package would pay off existing creditors (which in the main included benefactors from the club era who had maintained their support post-regionalisation), invest in the condition of the playing surface, and buy the whole ground, including the 'cabbage patch' behind one end of the pitch.

And then Dan Biggar – a loyal servant of the Ospreys for over a decade – announced that he had been tempted away to Northampton. Rumours circulated that his contract was worth as much as £600,000 per year. Whatever magic the union and the regions could work with NDCs, they could not compete with packages of that magnitude. A coach and horses had been driven through the terms of the rugby services agreement signed, after much excitement, in 2014. Worse, Biggar suggested that he was leaving for the opportunity to challenge for trophies, a less-than-subtle inference that he didn't think the Ospreys were likely to win anything any time soon.

Even so, the newly-buoyant Scarlets overcame a tricky start to their European campaign to rack up memorable wins away to Bath and home to Toulon before a rousing, memorable romp over La Rochelle in the Champions' Cup quarter-final. The semi-final away to Leinster was a step too far, as was a second consecutive appearance in the final of the domestic league, this time returning – unsuccessfully – to Lansdowne Road. Cardiff Blues, in the second-tier European Challenge Cup, picked up their second title with victory over Gloucester in Bilbao.

The WRU now turned its focus to governance reform. The 19-man WRU board – and it had been all men, until Aileen Richards was appointed in 2015 – was reduced to twelve in the autumn of 2018. In addition to the independent members who had been first appointed in 2015, the community and professional games would be separated for the first time, with both having sub-boards of their own, and the chairs of both the Community Game Board (CGB) and the Professional Rugby Board (PRB) gaining seats on the full WRU board. Five elected district representatives and two national council members would be elected by the member clubs.[9]

Yet the financial forecast remained bleak. In early 2019, rumours began to circulate of discussions within the PRB which had been given the working title 'Project Reset'. Under discussion were issues including a reset of the PRB with independent members, salary bands for players to ward off suitors in England and France, and the potential for differentiating between payments made to each of the four clubs.

A two-day meeting was convened to thrash out the details. Before those present had finished their coffees, the Ospreys' delegation set a hare running: 'Then it all started, kicked off by the Ospreys, "It's got to be three teams in south Wales, one in north Wales, and we're prepared to merge with the Scarlets," I nearly fell off my chair,' said Gareth Davies.[10]

The agenda for the rest of the two-day session was ripped up as the discussion focused on exploring the potential of the proposal. As the meeting ended, the main agreed action was for the Ospreys and Scarlets to consider the possibility of a merger.

'We had an offer on the Wednesday,' adds Ron Jones. 'They'd obviously thought it through, they knew what they wanted to do – they understood they would have to play in Llanelli, they accepted that they would have a minority of the shares, so we weren't exactly giving up our identity for their benefit, they agreed they wanted to do the deal, and at the last minute Rob Davies said he didn't want to do it.'[11]

By the following week, the Ospreys were back with a new proposal. They were still prepared to consider a merger with another club, but now with Cardiff Blues.

All of this during a Six Nations campaign. A campaign which, despite the chaos, ended in a fourth Welsh Grand Slam in 15 seasons.

'There was a meeting then at the Vale,' recalls Gareth Davies. 'Mike James walked in... not a happy bunny... and he read out a statement, basically resigning [from PRB]. I don't know how much of a falling out there had been back at base. But he read out this statement, "I'm resigning, Rob [Davies] will be available on speaker to take my place if you so wish. Thank you, gentlemen," and so on. He went downstairs to his car, and within seconds Mark Killingley, the press officer, turned to me and said, "Bloody hell, have a look at this." This was just as Mike was going down the steps. He showed me a press statement from the Ospreys, from Mike James, saying he was resigning, slagging the union off. He'd just walked down the stairs saying "thanks boys", you know? He hadn't even got to his car.'[12]

The press release was scathing, referring to the discussions as 'project inept... an ill-judged, cavalier process' and an example of 'catastrophic mismanagement'.

The Ospreys then piled in behind their former chairman, attacking the WRU for its 'conflict of interests, the lack of appropriate transparency and adequate governance in the "Project Reset" process, as well as inducements by officers of the WRU for the regional side to commit further private funds to the game while acting against its interests.'

PRB fired back, saying that the statements by James and the Ospreys 'do not reconcile with the minuted meetings, actions and documented agreements that have taken place' and that, in fact, by 1 March, a heads of terms agreement had been reached between the Ospreys and Scarlets to merge.

The statement was released in the names of all members of the PRB with the exception of the Ospreys. Clearly, any notion of a merger involving the Ospreys and, for that matter, any inkling of a fully-professional north Wales region, was off.[13]

By the summer, tempers had settled, and a new Professional Rugby Agreement (PRA) based on partnership and co-operation was finalised. Benefactors – those wealthy fans who had propped up professional rugby since 1995 – were to be eased out. Directors' loans were converted into shares or written off. At this time, the WRU paid around £21m to the professional teams, £9m of which was generated by participation and broadcast deals to which the regions themselves were party. More money would be found – £2.4m more in total – to allow a differentiated funding model based on a set of criteria which would see the playing budget in three regions increased to around £6m.[14]

The national men's team went into the 2019 Rugby World Cup in unfamiliarly fine fettle. Grand Slam champions, they had – vanishingly briefly, but it did happen – topped the world rugby rankings for the first (and, so far, only) time in their history that August. Preparations were calm and organised. Suspiciously calm and organised. It could not, of course, last. As the squad made its final preparations for the first game of the tournament, it emerged that

Gatland's long-standing lieutenant, Rob Howley, had broken World Rugby's betting regulations. There would be an investigation and Howley was stood down for the tournament. Gatland was grateful for the way in which the WRU acted in immediately sending senior administrators to Japan: 'I had nothing but admiration for the way the WRU people conducted themselves in acting with great speed, clarity, and openness. There was no ducking or diving, no misinformation or hiding behind process.'[15]

Howley was eventually found to have placed 363 bets on over 1,100 matches, some of which involved Wales, and two of which featured bets on Wales players scoring tries in the matches in question. An 18-month ban followed, half of which was suspended.[16]

With Stephen Jones drafted in to look after the attack, a victory over Australia in the pool stages – a first victory at a World Cup over one of the three traditional southern hemisphere powers since 1987's third-place play-off – meant that Wales finished top of their pool for the first time since 1999. The quarter-final against France was going badly until a red card – sweet, sweet karma for 2011 – allowed Wales to squeak home. Injuries again blighted their progress, with the semi-final against South Africa decided in the final minutes. Wales were exhausted, with several players held together by sticky tape. Head coach Warren Gatland left at the end of the tournament, his record – two semi-finals and a quarter-final in his three tournaments, along with three Six Nations Grand Slams – an impressive legacy.

Back in Wales, there were the faintest rumblings that the administration was taking its first tentative steps into the mid-to-late twentieth century, just in time for the third decade of the twenty-first. Former national captain Liza Burgess became the first woman to be elected by the clubs as a national representative to the WRU board. Former Zurich and future Aviva executive Amanda Blanc was appointed chair of the

Professional Rugby Board, and therefore automatically took the PRB's seat on the full WRU board.

By the first month of the new decade, more change was in the air. Martyn Phillips, chief executive since 2015, announced his intention to step down in the summer. His chairman, Gareth Davies, having pushed through new rules which limited the chair to two, three-year terms, said that he would also step down at the autumn's annual general meeting.

On the field, new Wales coach Wayne Pivac's first Six Nations was testing. A convincing win over Italy, exhibiting the Scarlets' ambitious style which had made Pivac a popular choice for the role in the first place, provided a decent start. The now-traditional chastening defeat in Ireland followed, while the home game against resurgent France saw the visitors triumph in Cardiff for the first time since 2010 (although Wales were within a scrambling French tackle of a last-minute winning score). A – again, by now, traditional – rousing comeback at Twickenham when all seemed lost again fell just short in a 33–30 defeat.

The final game of the championship, scheduled for the following Saturday against Scotland in Cardiff, would be postponed. Covid had arrived, and nothing would ever be quite the same.

CHAPTER 9

Pandemic and Penury

'In her leaving speech, Blanc recalled a "truly offensive discussion" about reducing the sanctions for an elected WRU member after he had made misogynistic comments in public, including that "men are the master race" and women should "stick to the ironing".

"I've been in business for a long period of time, but when you are just simply not listened to, some misogynistic comments. There was one which was 'what do you know about governance?' Well, quite a lot actually. I've got 32 years of experience and I operate in a regulated business. Nobody else was asked that question, but I was. I got an apology for that actually, a written apology for it."'[1]

(BBC report on an appearance by Amanda Blanc, former PRB Chair, on BBC Radio 4's *Desert Island Discs*, March 2023)

THE SURREAL NATURE of 2020 is now sometimes difficult to recall. Until March, the population of the UK watched the unfolding horror, from their living rooms, as the pandemic spread from Asia to Europe. They saw images of the collapsing health system in northern Italy while the UK's prime minister walked around hospitals here, minus a facemask, merrily shaking hands with everybody he came across.

As far as that spring's Six Nations championship was concerned, everything carried on as normal for the first four rounds of matches. Wales travelled to Twickenham on the penultimate weekend, as Martyn Phillips recalled: 'Boris Johnson attended the England game, which was clearly a statement that not only had he allowed the match to go ahead but he was happy to attend himself. We were actually sat on the same table as him talking about nothing else other than Covid. Nobody was shaking hands. That weekend was the start of the elbow bump.'

The medical advice from the Welsh government remained that open-air gatherings were safe. The Scottish team, and most of the supporters who would follow them on their biennial trek to Cardiff, were already in town by the Friday. And then the cancellations started. All football was cancelled across the UK, golfing events in the USA and motor-racing in Australia too.

Gareth Davies recalls: 'Some of the journalists were pulling my leg saying you are going to get amazing viewing figures this weekend because you are the only sport happening in Europe.'

By the Friday lunchtime, the match had been postponed. The Welsh government health minister Vaughan Gething said that: 'WRU found themselves in a pretty extraordinary position,' but said the 'medical advice about the risk to people going to the rugby didn't change. What did change was the fact that the rest of the sporting world decided that, regardless of that advice, they wanted to put off events.'[2]

The WRU may have hoped to play the game a few weeks later once the pandemic was under control, but rugby would not be played in front of full stadia again in Wales for another 19 months. Indeed, the Principality Stadium and Parc y Scarlets were both used as field hospitals for the remainder of 2020 (in Parc y Scarlets' case, moving indoors to the training barn in the autumn).

The sport, already struggling financially, now faced ruin. The tens of millions of pounds generated by Six Nations and autumn matches hadn't been generated in all that time.

In the circumstances, Martyn Phillips agreed to delay his departure from the WRU chief executive officer's role from early 2020 to the end of the year. One possible salvation lay in the interest which venture capitalists CVC were showing in the sport. By May 2020, Celtic Rugby DAC – which owned the league then known as the Pro14 – sold a 28% stake in the competition to CVC. The WRU, as one of the owners of Celtic Rugby DAC, would receive approximately £33m over five years. A few months later, CVC also acquired a 14.7% stake in the Six Nations – worth around £51m to the WRU.

Gareth Davies had driven through reforms – cutting the WRU board from 19 members to twelve, and imposing term limits so that newly-elected WRU board members could serve no more than three three-year terms, and no more than two three-year terms as chair. Coming to the end of his second term as both a board member and chair, he was persuaded to stand for election one more time, and to put himself forward as chair for a third term.

Former Wales internationals Ieuan Evans and Nigel Davies stood against Davies as a national representative to the WRU board.

In his autobiography, Ieuan had written damningly of the influence of community clubs on the elite game: 'How could you have officials from small clubs with no real knowledge of world rugby making decisions which affected the national team and, more often than not, affected it for the worse?... Democracy is all very well but too many small clubs have too big a say without having any knowledge of what is entailed at international level. The WRU have a lot to answer for. Too narrow in its outlook for far too long, it has been guilty of a disturbing lack of foresight and guilty on too many occasions of behaving with a serious lack of dignity.'[3]

In the intervening 25 years or so, he had clearly developed an acute political antenna, as he made his pitch to individual clubs. Many community clubs spoke of his readiness to contact each of them. He also, in his written pitch to the clubs, promised them the earth.

Davies wrote to the clubs: 'Please don't underestimate the impact and the repercussions of a vote for one of the other two candidates in this race. It is highly likely there would be a sea-change in the direction of travel and strategic objectives of the Welsh Rugby Union. We would be entering unknown territory, and at a time like this, is this really wise?'[4]

At the October 2020 AGM, Davies was defeated by Ieuan Evans, who was himself immediately installed as the WRU board vice-chairman. Rob Butcher, a retired teacher, was elected chair. Martyn Phillips also departed as CEO at the AGM to be replaced – initially on an interim, and then permanent basis – by long-serving finance director Steve Phillips.

It was, in the words of Ron Jones, 'the revenge of the blazers... Gareth [Davies] gave it his best shot – when he came up with changes, they voted them down and they threw him out.'[5]

The long-awaited conclusion of 'Project Reset', with the agreement of a new PRA, had seen the benefactors write off the £70m plus they had poured into the professional game in Wales over the previous 25 years. Peter Thomas, at Cardiff, personally wrote off or converted into loans an eye-watering £14m.[6]

As part of the agreement, WRU payments would increase substantially. For the 2020–21 season, the payment to be made by the WRU to the four regions was expected to be in the region of £26.6m, the increase in large part due to the establishment of a list of 38 elite players who would in effect have 80% of their costs covered by the WRU, with the remaining 20% covered by their region. The purpose of this element was to make the retention of Test players – who would routinely spend around half the season away with Wales – more attractive to regions who would rarely see them. 'Expected to be,' because the nature of the agreement meant that the WRU would ring-fence funding for certain elements – for instance, the community game would be guaranteed £11.6m per year – with the Professional Rugby Board receiving whatever was left over. The intention being that it would bring a risk and reward element to the professional game and drive income generation across the five bodies – the four professional teams and the union.

It quickly became apparent that the deal ensured that the professional teams were the ones taking all the risk.

The 2021 Six Nations – in which Wales, helped by an improbable series of red cards against their opponents, were champions but had the Grand Slam snatched from their grasp well into injury time in the final game in Paris – was played in completely empty stadia. The game's finances took another hit.

With turnover falling from £90.5m in 2019 to £58.1m in 2021, the WRU decided to stick to the letter of the PRA, ignoring a clause which allowed variation in exceptional circumstances (a clause which, some might argue, a once-in-a-century global pandemic fitted). The community clubs would be protected and would receive the full £11.6m. The four professional teams, meanwhile, would see their expected £26.6m payment reduced to £3.6m. The WRU would not pay for the release of players for international games, yet the regions were still obliged – under the terms of the PRA – to release them.

The union sought a loan to cover their non-payment. Initially, they misunderstood the nature of the devolution settlement, believing that the RFU would lead on negotiations with the UK government's Department for Culture, Media, and Sport. When UK government announced a £300m support package, with £135m set aside for rugby, it took a while for the realisation to sink in that it was for English rugby only. A £20m loan (£2m from World Rugby, £18m from NatWest's Coronavirus large business interruption loan scheme (CLBILS)) for Welsh rugby was quickly secured by the WRU – to, let's remember, cover its payments to the professional clubs – the bulk of which it decided the clubs would repay over three years.

Acting CEO Steve Phillips then told the BBC that he expected that the Welsh government would support Welsh rugby to the tune of around £30m–£40m. It eventually managed to refinance the loan via an agreement with the Welsh government over a longer repayment term, but the debt remained on the regions' books.

'There isn't a recognition from the WRU that risk needs to be shared amongst the whole economy of Welsh rugby,' says Huw Jones of supporters' trust CF10. 'In other words, the WRU plus the four regions. The then Governor of the Bank of England made this point when he visited Wales once, and the then CEO of the WRU, Roger Lewis, was present. The WRU has an attitude which is "Well, actually, we need to devolve our risk, because we mustn't go bust – if they go bust, it doesn't matter, we'll just set something else up." So, there's that very simplistic attitude. That's a fundamental issue... the regions are carrying all of the risk and they're getting none of the reward. They thought before that they were going to get all the rewards. So, they have to take some responsibility for signing up to the contract, but I think the WRU should also think "Well, actually, it's not a fair contract any more and we have to change it... the risk has to be shared better".'[7]

Mark Evans – erstwhile CEO of clubs such as Saracens and Harlequins, and back in 2006 in the running for the Wales head coach job – didn't understand the WRU's approach: 'To load up the regions with even more debt during a pandemic strikes me as almost inexplicable. I just don't get it. It puts those regions, who have lost their crowds to a significant degree and are struggling on the pitch... You try and turn any club around on and off the pitch while battling a financial crisis – good luck.'[8]

Shane Williams went further: 'The compromise is always

made in Wales on behalf of the national team because they are deemed to be the cash cow for the whole game here. But in so doing the WRU actively work against the viability of the four regions, who are regularly shorn of their best players and who haven't been able to perform to their best ability in their domestic league or Europe.'[9]

But what had happened to the near £90m windfall, over five years, from CVC's investment in Celtic Rugby and the Six Nations?

The WRU decided to treat the sale to CVC as a capital receipt, and further decided that they would use the money not to better support its rugby supply chain, but to invest in longer-term possibilities which, it hoped, would provide long-term and reliable income. It invested in a hotel on Westgate Street which opened in October 2021. It has also explored rather more eccentric ideas such as a stadium roofwalk and zip wire.[10] While the roofwalk has yet to leave the drawing board, the WRU have recently announced a multi-million pound joint venture to build a zip wire attraction on the roof of the national stadium. It is understood that this will be partly funded from money received from CVC.

The women's national team lost every game in its 2021 Six Nations, prompting the WRU to commission a mid-term performance review. Wales remained an amateur team, drawing its players mostly from the English league. The gulf to the professional English and French teams was vast, and widening. Jasmine Joyce, a superstar of the Sevens game and a fixture in the Wales XV team, talked of the possibility of having to give up rugby once her GB Sevens contract expired at the end of the delayed Tokyo Olympics in 2021. Over 120 former Wales players wrote a joint letter to the WRU demanding a change in the union's approach to the women's game. A 4,000-signature petition followed.

By the autumn, while the review remained unpublished, the WRU undertook to offer the first fully professional contracts in the history of women's rugby in the country. To ten players. A further 15 would be offered twelve-month 'retainer' contracts. No more would be heard of the review's recommendation until the summer of 2023, when a list of 40 recommendations were shared by the WRU with the Senedd's Culture, Communications, Welsh Language, Sport and International Relations Committee.[11]

Amidst financial uncertainty, the PRB sought to provide a semblance of stability with an agreement on – indicative – figures for the next two years. Subject to the WRU hitting its financial targets – that risk/reward element again – the professional teams would receive payments of £23m for the 2021–22 season, and £23.5m for the following season.

During the 2010s, the relative success of the national men's team had papered over the widening cracks within the game in Wales. By 2022, they had become increasingly difficult to ignore. Wales, champions in 2021, lost at home to Italy for the first time in the Six Nations. An unlikely win in Bloemfontein – a first-ever for Wales in South Africa – provided a brief respite for embattled head coach Wayne Pivac. But a disastrous autumn series, culminating in a defeat to Georgia which echoed the defeat to Romania nearly 25 years earlier, led to a volley of wailing and teeth-gnashing. Pivac and his coaching team were sacked, and Warren Gatland returned.

The regions played a series of eight games against South African provinces that spring, newly incorporated into the Pro14 to create the United Rugby Championship. All eight were lost – with not even the consolation of a losing bonus point – and an average margin of defeat of 31 points. Sean Everitt, coach at the Durban-based Sharks, at least had the consideration to note that there was a marked difference between playing the Welsh regions in the northern autumn – when teams were close to full-strength – and playing those same teams mid Six Nations when denuded of their internationals, painfully exposing their lack of depth.

Yet even when fully loaded, the regions struggled. Their decline was obvious. In the ten years since the Ospreys' most recent domestic triumph in 2012, only the Scarlets in 2017 had won the title. In Europe's top competition, only the Scarlets – once, in 2017–18 – had even managed to reach the quarter-finals.[12]

'Welsh rugby is broken, and there doesn't seem to be a plan to fix it,' opined the *Western Mail*'s Matthew Southcombe. 'The tail wags the dog,' he went on, citing the influence of community clubs on the elite game.[13]

The Professional Rugby Board commissioned an evaluation of the state of the elite game and its potential options, colloquially known as the Oakwell report. Its findings were stark. The Irish Rugby Football Union, it estimated, invested €50–60m in its four professional provinces, while the Scottish Rugby Union spent around £20m on its two professional teams. It foresaw that the PRB budget would reduce from £23.5m in 2023 to around £18m by 2024. A funding gap of around £7m was forecast, with potential solutions including cutting player salaries by over 12%, cutting squad sizes by 10%, and even closing one of the four regions to realise an anticipated saving of £7.8m.

'You reap what you sow,' said David Moffett in response, 'and the WRU have neglected the professional game for a number of years. It didn't have to be this way, but this is where we are currently at, and there's only enough money for three sides. The WRU has been underfunding professional rugby in my view to get one of the professional teams to fold. They haven't done that, so now they are going down this other track that they get some independent advice to say we have to go down to three if we are going to survive this financial crisis.'[14]

By the autumn of 2022, a new six-year agreement had been put before the PRB by the WRU. Summed up by the journalist Steffan Thomas as, 'WRU Tell Regions: "Here's £30m For Your

Players... It's Mostly a Loan, And Your Money Men Have to Carry the Risk",'[15] it made for grim reading. Some of the CVC money would be used to support payments to the professional teams.

Ron Jones was unimpressed: 'In my view it's an economic madhouse... Not even a corner shop would be run in that way... The idea that we now design a business model for Welsh rugby which involves ensuring the supply of quality players to the national team, whilst making benefactors pay for that, is the equivalent of a company in any business which claims to be successful and profitable only because it receives charitable donations from external people on a regular basis.'[16]

The new year started in familiar fashion, with supporters of the four regions protesting at the traditional derbies. 'Save Our Game' was the cry, in part at least to the union's refusal to meet with the Joint Supporters Group for well over a year.

A bad start to the year for the WRU. But it would get much, much worse.

Early in 2022, the *Daily Mail*'s Liz Perkins and Alex Bywater wrote about a – then – unnamed WRU employee who had left the organisation after being subjected to misogynistic comments, including one comparing her to Hitler, and 'jokes' by a male colleague about wanting to 'rape her'. By the summer, Perkins reported on an employment tribunal which had made further allegations of misogynistic behaviour and the use of casually racist language. A senior figure within the union was said to have dismissed the women's game, suggesting that the WRU didn't need to focus on professionalising it.

It took almost a year for the story to achieve genuine cut-through, with the airing of a *BBC Wales Investigates* programme in January 2023 in which Charlotte Wathan spoke openly about her treatment at the hands of colleagues within the WRU. Others supported the suggestion that the culture within the union was deeply unhealthy; another unnamed former employee said that she had felt suicidal, others outlined examples of casual misogyny, racism, and homophobia. One former press officer recalled that she had not been permitted to sit in an all-male committee meeting about which she was expected to draft a press release – her male manager had to sit near the door and whisper key points of the discussion to her as she sat outside.

Amanda Blanc, Aviva Group CEO, who had resigned as the PRB's chair in late 2021 for unspecified reasons – in public, at least – now broke cover during an appearance on the BBC's *Desert Island Discs*. She recalled being ignored and not listened to by WRU board members. One asked her what she knew about governance – a comment for which she received a written apology. In a leaving speech – delivered to the WRU but not, apparently, recalled by the people it was delivered to – she noted a 'truly offensive discussion' about reducing the sanctions for an elected WRU member after he had made misogynistic comments in public, including that 'men are the master race' and women should 'stick to the ironing'.

'I still feel that genuinely, and I don't say this very often, if I had been listened to then we wouldn't have had the situation that would have happened over the last number of weeks, particularly in respect of the women's game. There was a women's review which was undertaken about the way that women were treated very differently to men. I called for the women's review to be made public and I called for the board's governance to be modernised, neither of those two things have happened and we find ourselves now in the situation where a lot of women have come forward to say that they were badly treated. It left me feeling deeply frustrated, very sad actually.'[17]

The tone of the WRU's response appeared to minimise the seriousness of the accusations. Warren Gatland spoke of his ignorance of the events, but offered the view that there were often two sides to every story. Attempts to portray both sides allegedly included the release of information about one of the complainants by the WRU. Steve Phillips wrote to member clubs, suggesting that the issues covered in the programme had arisen between 2017 and 2019. In other words, before Phillips was appointed CEO. He had, however, been the WRU's finance director for over 15 years.

Hayley Parsons, a director at Cardiff Rugby, was furious, writing of a 'long-standing and deep-rooted culture of toxicity and bullying within the WRU'. Welsh rugby, she wrote, was 'fundamentally broken from top to bottom... Supporters of Mr Phillips and certain members of the WRU board are now closing ranks and linking arms, protecting the few to the detriment of the majority. We have to break this chain. The current situation is not acceptable and is untenable. There has to be immediate change and action.'[18]

Ron Jones at the Scarlets wasn't surprised by the revelations: 'I've come across some examples of bullying in rugby, but not that many. But within the union it was strong. And I don't remember it in the days of Vernon Pugh, Glanmor Griffiths, David Moffett. But it built up during the years when Team Wales was everything.'[19]

Phillips eventually stepped down, to be replaced on an interim basis by former Wales international, and then WRU performance director, Nigel Walker. Among the new CEO's first duties was an appearance before a Senedd committee with his chair, Ieuan Evans, where he recognised that the union had been in denial about its problematic culture. Walker soon set up an independent inquiry into the allegations under the leadership of Dame Anne Rafferty and including former England international Maggie Alphonsi and former English Premiership Rugby chair Quentin Smith. It is due to report later in 2023.

Back on the field, Wales started the Six Nations with a heavy home defeat to Ireland, followed by a record defeat away to Scotland, the 35–7 margin eclipsing the 35–10 reverse of 1922 (although admittedly a try had been worth only three points at the time).

Before the third game of the championship, stories began to circulate that the national squad's players were considering strike action. The contracts of over 70 professional players were due to expire at the end of the season, and the endless delays in securing a new financial agreement within the PRB meant that the teams – not knowing their budgets for the 2023–24 season – were unable to offer new terms. However, rumours circulated – since proven correct – that squad budgets would be cut from between £6m–£7m in 2022–23, to a maximum of £5.2m in 2023–24 and £4.5m in 2024–25.

Players began to speak out. One revealed that he was taking anti-depressants. Another had been unable to secure a mortgage. Another, now based outside Wales but a regular Test player, said that he had no desire to come back to Wales to play. Another said that he had never known it to be this bad. Yet another had put his home up for sale and had moved back in with his parents as he had no certainty that he would be able to keep a roof over his head in the current climate.

Before the England game, players turned up for, and promptly walked out from, a pre-match function at the WRU's Parkgate Hotel, citing their frustration at the uncertainty of their situations.

At Cardiff, it emerged that a number of senior players – many earning between £100,000 and £250,000 – had been told that the best the club could do for them would be new deals worth around £30,000. In some cases, players were told that the club didn't want to insult them by offering even that amount.

Days before the England game, an interim agreement was reached. The game would go ahead, but the players' representative body, the Welsh Rugby Players Association (WRPA) would gain a seat at the PRB table, the controversial fixed/variable elements of new standardised contracts would become optional, the 60-cap rule (which prevented players playing outside Wales from being selected for the national team unless they had already won 60 caps) would be reduced to 25, and players would have the right to reject loan moves. The game may have been played – and lost – but the financial issues remained unresolved. Despite acting CEO Nigel Walker's comments prior to the game that he would hold the regions' feet to the fire unless they started re-contracting players, the professional teams remained unable to do so with no formal agreement in place. It wouldn't arrive until the end of March. In any case, payments by the WRU to the regions were delayed – the complex series of loans negotiated by the WRU during the pandemic meant that the new six-year PRA required sign-off from several external bodies – and regional benefactors had to cover salaries themselves late in the season without WRU support.

Players were forced to leave their clubs. Many were fortunate enough to be offered deals in England, France, Japan and New Zealand. But, with the regions now less able to recruit and retain national team players, their availability to Wales became an issue. Ross Moriarty signed for relegation-threatened Brive, asking not to be considered for Wales' Rugby World Cup preparations. Senior players such as Alun Wyn Jones and Justin Tipuric announced their retirements from international rugby, several weeks after being named in the expanded Rugby World Cup training squad. Rhys Webb took up an offer at Biarritz which meant that he would not be available to play at the tournament. Cory Hill, having indicated his wish to return from Japan and to restart his Test career, was unable to secure a playing contract in Wales and had to re-sign for a club in Japan, which meant that he too would be unavailable. The young centre Joe Hawkins had been capped by Wayne Pivac while still on a development contract at the Ospreys and had retained his place under Gatland through much of the Six Nations. He had already agreed to join Exeter but believed that he would remain eligible for Wales. He was mistaken, and his Test career will, unless the policy changes, be on hold for the next few years. Others – including Leigh Halfpenny – remained clubless as they prepared for the showpiece event.

An attempt had been made in 2022 to push through governance changes, but these had failed to secure the necessary 75% supermajority of club support. The WRU finally secured changes which would later see barrister and former PwC vice-chair Richard Collier-Keywood appointed as its first independent chair. Other changes agreed at the March 2023 EGM included the reduction of the number of elected club representatives on the WRU board from eight to four, an increase in the number of independent non-executive directors from three to six, and an 'ambition' that its composition would be changed so that 40% of its members are women.

As the national team stepped up its World Cup preparations, rumours emerged yet again of a proposed reduction in the number of professional teams. And yet again, it was the Ospreys who were at the centre of most of them. There were rumours of a merger with Cardiff, Ealing Trailfinders and two English clubs which had disappeared the previous season, Wasps and London Irish. Those two were also rumoured to be considering buying Zebre Parma's franchise so that they could join the URC. David Moffett popped up again to suggest that the WRU should move heaven and earth to take advantage of the demise of Wasps, London Irish and Worcester Warriors by pushing for the creation of an Anglo-Welsh League.

'This has got to be the most tumultuous season in terms of everything that's happened on and off the field,' says Alex Bywater, in an echo of John Billot's words 30 years ago, of the 2022–23 season. 'But it feels like Welsh rugby got razed to the ground. My hope is this is sort of ground zero. While no one would have wanted to get to this stage, it could be an opportunity to rebuild a better organisation for the good of Welsh rugby. There are so many passionate people in the game and it's still so important to the nation.'[20]

CHAPTER 10

The Road to Redemption?

'Perhaps, like an ill-conceived hotel buffet plate, it is not the individual components that are the problem but the sheer ambition of the operation itself. Perhaps – and I'm going out on a limb here – running a World Cup campaign, running an Under-11s league, devising a funding settlement for the professional game and building a zip wire are largely different jobs for largely different people.'[1]

(Jonathan Liew, 'Strike threats and Netflix feuds: Wales's rugby crisis exposes greater problem', *The Guardian*, 20 February 2023)

THE 2023 EDITION of the men's Rugby World Cup, in France, was a welcome distraction.

The flickering signs of improvement in the August preparatory games against England gave way to something more substantial. Wales were inconsistent, but, at their best, clinical.

With co-captain Dewi Lake working his way back to fitness, it fell to Cwmtwrch's Jac Morgan to confirm his burgeoning reputation as both a Test player and captain. A game for the ages with Fiji ran the France–New Zealand opener close for the match of that first weekend. Josh Adams' tackle on Selestino Ravutaumada was one of its most memorable moments. Wales set off like a train, a midfield break by George North eventually leading to an early try for Adams. Back came Fiji with tries of their own as their physicality threatened to overwhelm Wales. An Elliot Dee try from a lineout drive to make it 32–14 after 67 minutes secured the bonus point and seemed to have put the game to bed. But Fiji weren't done. An irresistible wave of attacks in the final ten minutes brought them two tries. The eight-try thriller was finally secured for Wales thanks to an almost inexplicable dropped pass by Semi Radradra, with the line at his mercy, on the last play.

A stuttering performance against Portugal – put into context by Os Lobos' wonderful showing throughout the pool stages – followed. It took Wales until the dying seconds to secure the expected fourth try for the bonus point – Taulupe Faletau, in what may well be his last Rugby World Cup, decided to do it all himself. But it was job done.

Australia – for the fifth time in seven Rugby World Cup pool stages – were up next. If the fixture was familiar, the result certainly wasn't. Wales played with a cold-eyed fury. A wonderful opening try by Gareth Davies after two minutes set the tone. Australia were throttled – a penalty on 14 minutes proved to be their final score of the game. Despite their dominance, Wales retained their composure. When the Wallabies transgressed, they kicked the points. When there was nothing on, Gareth Anscombe dropped a goal. The lead built and built and built. Only in the final minutes, 29 points ahead, did Wales turn down a kickable penalty, go to the corner and drive over. The final score was 40–6 – the kind of scoreline which for many years was routine in this match-up, albeit usually – at least since the mid-1970s – the other way around. It was Wales' record victory margin over Australia. It was also Australia's worst ever Rugby World Cup defeat.

Another stumbling if (almost) always comfortable victory

over Georgia – made safe by a Louis Rees-Zammit hat-trick – concluded the pool stages. For the second successive tournament – and only the third time in ten World Cups – Wales had won every pool-stage game.

The draw appeared to have opened up, with their quarter-final opponents scheduled to be the runners-up in Pool D. It could have been England. In the event, it was Argentina, who had started the tournament so badly that they played 78 minutes against 14 Englishmen and contrived to lose 27–10 (and it was only that close thanks to Bruni's last-minute consolation try).

In traditional fashion, Welsh fans got carried away and started thinking about which of Ireland or New Zealand they might play in the semi-finals. And, given the path those two teams had been forced to negotiate by an unbalanced draw, there was every chance that whichever of those teams emerged from their quarter-final later that evening would be exhausted. So maybe there would be a chance. And then it might be South Africa or France, both of whom had tough journeys through the tournament, or maybe even England, and, well, they couldn't, could they?

They couldn't.

A nervous first ten minutes opened up into a complete display. Wales were disciplined, ambitious, creative and dangerous, stretching and stressing the Argentina defence. For 20 minutes. A glorious try finished by Dan Biggar opened up a lead. Penalties mounted up, but – unlike the Australia game – kicks at goal were turned down. The resulting lineouts malfunctioned. An almost resigned shrug of a decision to take a straightforward shot at goal, to make it 13–0, was missed. On 37 minutes, it was still 10–0 to Wales. By half-time, it was 10–6. Eight minutes into the second half, Wales were behind. A Tomos Williams snipe put them five points up again, but it was completely against the run of play. Argentina emptied their bench, Wales did likewise, but it was Wales who ran out of steam. A try twelve minutes from time put Argentina back ahead, and when, with two minutes left, Wales tried a desperate loop play on the back foot in their own half, the veteran Nicolás Sánchez intercepted to win the game.

In hindsight, Wales looked exhausted. They had again placed great faith in their fitness and were happy to use a kicking game to pressurise opponents into errors. It had worked across the pool stages, and they looked better organised than for some time. But it was a physically demanding approach. They made 168 tackles in that quarter-final, and nine of the top eleven tacklers were Welsh. Across their five games, they made 837 tackles, an average of 167 per game. In comparison, the next highest tackle count among the quarter-finalists was South Africa's 656, or 131 per game. Wales had made a full game's-worth of tackles more than any other team in the tournament to that point. In the Fiji game, they made a Rugby World Cup record 253 tackles, 27 of which were made by Will Rowlands (with Gareth Thomas and Jac Morgan also making 20-plus). Fifteen Welsh players – including Sam Costelow, who was only on the field for 13 minutes – made more tackles than any single Fijian.

In an echo of the previous two campaigns, the squad were picking up injuries at the business end of the tournament. On their return, Warren Gatland confirmed that, of the team which had started against Argentina, both half-backs and the entire back three wouldn't have been available for the following week's semi-final had Wales made it. Taulupe Faletau was already out of the tournament with a broken arm. Doubts persisted over the fitness of a number of other players. A semi-final against a resurgent New Zealand could have been a significant step too far. As, indeed, it was for Argentina, who were fortunate not to take Wales' unwanted record for the heaviest ever semi-final defeat.

Nevertheless, they had disproved the pessimists who doubted that they could escape such a tough group.

A quarter-final for a Six Nations or Rugby Championship team is about par. Given performances on the pitch over the previous two years, it was perhaps better than par.

***

In his first post-World Cup press conference back in Wales, Gatland spoke positively about the progress made by the squad. There were signs of an understanding that the national men's team could no longer thrive without a functioning professional tier. During the 2023 Six Nations Gatland had recognised that the regions had been underfunded, hinting at a dawning realisation that the professional teams were, after all, important.

'Now I look back on the first period I was here, a lot of these issues were going on but the fact we had been reasonably successful probably papered over the cracks a little bit. It was stopping the dam from bursting. The dam has burst now. It's burst because the regions feel they are underfunded. As a national side we're not being successful. The desire to play for Wales and be in Wales potentially isn't as strong as it was. Winning often hides away the issues that are going on behind the scenes.'[2]

Hope for the future? For a more constructive relationship between all levels of the Welsh game? For co-operation? Fat chance.

Almost as soon as the Rugby World Cup squad touched down back home, another squad was announced. Because the WRU had arranged yet another international game. It would be a farewell to Alun Wyn Jones, who would be invited to represent the Barbarians against Wales on 4 November. The same day that the Scarlets were due to entertain Cardiff at Parc y Scarlets. One of the few 'event' games in the domestic calendar. One of the few which draws any away supporters at all. One of the few opportunities the regions have to attract a good crowd, take advantage of a rare prime-time kick-off slot, and bring in the kind of self-generated income that the Oakwell report felt would reduce regional reliance on WRU payments. All the more important in this of all seasons, with budgets slashed, squads weakened, and very little prospect of any success for any of the Welsh teams.

So, of course, the union decided to schedule a meaningless match for the national team 60 miles up the M4 on the same day, nabbing for themselves many star names who should have been turning out for their regions.

Nigel Walker – as the WRU's still-acting chief executive – at least accepted the union's mistake, admitting that, when URC fixtures were agreed, the union should have stated that 4 November clashed with a Test match and that a Welsh derby on that date was out of the question. Yet, of course, nothing was done to change the situation, beyond promises that lessons would be learned, and that such a conflict would not happen again. At least separate discussions – this time to host a Bristol home game at the Principality Stadium on the same December day that the Scarlets and Cardiff were due to have their return match next door at Cardiff Arms Park – were discreetly shelved. But then, a few days later, it was reported that the now annual Judgement Day – in which two Welsh derbies are played as a double-header at the Principality Stadium – would have to find a new venue in 2024. The reason? The stadium had been double-booked, and another event would take precedence.

***

Throughout this book, we have seen that public perception of the state of the game can sometimes be overwhelmingly guided by the fortunes of the men's national team. In the late 1990s, Wales were among the whipping boys of international rugby, which led to a push towards recruiting miracle-working coaches from New Zealand and then, when that didn't work, to a reduction in the number of teams. Throughout the 2000s, the fortunes of the national team and the senior professional teams seemed to be linked – struggling at the start of the decade, blooming towards its middle and end. From around 2010, the balance between the two tiers was tipped significantly in favour of the national team. It flourished, but the professional teams withered. And yet, because Wales were racking up the Grand Slams and Championships and World Cup semi-final appearances, a plurality, if not a majority, of Welsh rugby supporters were content.

Finally, in 2022, the scales started to fall from the eyes of the Welsh rugby public. Once the men's national team stopped winning, everything else began to be questioned. First-ever home defeats to Italy and Georgia will tend to have that effect.

It was into this context that the poor overall health of the game, and in particular stories about the culture of the Welsh Rugby Union, finally began to make some headway.

The focus of this book has been mainly on the elite men's game. Some of the issues which exploded into the public consciousness in 2023 deserve their own books, and there isn't the space here to do them justice. Nevertheless, the preoccupation with power which has so beset the development of the elite men's game feeds through into the alleged culture of misogyny, racism and homophobia exposed in recent times.

Huw Jones has experience of power structures within the WRU and similar organisations after his time with the Sports Council for Wales: 'With all the resources that rugby has had over the years... there has been a huge failure of the structure and of the system – that is in many ways the biggest indictment. And it's ironic that it's the misogyny and homophobia and sexism that's actually now brought down the structure, because it could have been the lack of development... When you look at the problems that have occurred recently – misogyny, homophobia, sexism – those sorts of allegations – that comes from an organisation which is beset by a culture of arrogance and power. That's what those issues are. They're about power. People don't think about things like that, but they know it in the back of their minds.'[3]

The game in Wales has long been accused of mistreating those it might think of as less powerful. We have already explored the WRU's – and its clubs' – ambivalent attitude towards apartheid-era South Africa. Tales about apparently casually racist comments in recent years would come as no surprise to those who remember the 1980s. Two of the highest profile black players in the Welsh game at that time were Glenn Webbe and Gerald Cordle, wingers – and it is interesting to note that a 1994 survey of the Welsh leagues found that two-thirds of black players played on the wing[4] – at Bridgend and Cardiff respectively. Both were subjected to racist abuse – Webbe had bananas thrown at him during matches, Cordle once climbed into the crowd during a Cup match at Aberavon Quins as a result of comments directed at him by a spectator. In earlier times, young black men who would become legends of rugby league felt compelled to leave Wales, and the union game, because they did not expect to be equitably treated here. Indeed, it wasn't until 1983 that a black player was capped by the national team, and it would be another 20 years before a black player would be appointed captain.

Neither would the mistreatment of female employees, and of the women's game more generally, come as a surprise to many. The centrality of rugby to the emerging Welsh national identity of the early twentieth century has been briefly discussed in a previous chapter, but it was a 'masculine world where sexism flourished on the pitch and in the clubhouse' suggests Martin Johnes, adding that 'women remain marginal within the culture of those sports and thus the national identity that they project. Furthermore, as sexual discrimination increasingly became socially unacceptable, sport could even act as something of a last bastion of traditional ideas of male domination and gender roles.'[5] As late as 1993, the *Observer* felt it appropriate to write about Wales' unlikely victory over England as follows: 'Once it has sunk in today, the singing in the chapels will be heavenly and afterwards the pubs will be joyfully overflowing and the Welsh womenfolk will be baking their Welsh cakes and taking their men to their bosoms.'[6]

The stories which emerged during the last year about the way senior figures in the Welsh game viewed the women's game suggest that it has quite a way to go. The 2021 review into the women's game, part-published in 2023, indicated a serious problem.

'The review made very challenging reading for us,' wrote Nigel Walker, 'and described a committed squad of high-performance athletes frustrated by the support they were receiving, with failures in strategic and operational management, and not enough care, resource and encouragement for our international players to perform at their best. The review report also made clear that we had not ensured that our female players felt fully welcomed, valued and an equal part of our game.'[7]

Early days, but there are signs that the problem is at last being acknowledged by the WRU. More professional contracts were awarded in 2023 to supplement those awarded a year earlier. The backroom team has been augmented by new appointments. From a whitewash in 2020, Six Nations performances had improved sufficiently by 2023 to ensure qualification for a new global tournament, the WXV. And in the first tier, too, where Wales faced the best in the world in New Zealand this autumn. Wales' elite players now have two annual blocks of international fixtures in the form of the Six Nations and WXV.

Yet there is still much to do. With the demise of some English clubs, particularly Worcester Warriors, many leading

Welsh players find themselves competing in the WXV without a club contract. There is no professional women's rugby in Wales – whether it is wise to expect clubs in the country next door to develop our elite players is a debate which will need to be had.

The union's treatment of its male players has been little better.

'Welsh rugby's product is the teams and the teams are made up of the players. If you don't look after the players – and this doesn't mean they should get everything they ask for – then what are you left with?' asked Alex Bywater, reflecting on the threatened player strike during the 2023 Six Nations. 'They are professional, they're still being paid, but they're ultimately still employees. If you didn't know where you were going to be working in two months' time, you'd probably have doubts or worries or things occupying your mind. I think we expect sports people just to get on with it and be immune to some of these things. And it's quite clear that they weren't.'[8]

Warren Gatland's reaction to the threatened strike action in February 2023 appeared to be a little cloth-eared, suggesting that the players were behaving impulsively, going as far as hinting at splits in the Wales camp over the dispute which had caused tensions.

The players were asking not for more money, but for security and to be treated with dignity. The union had, after all, found the money to dispense with its previous coaching regime and to install a new set-up at a substantial cost. It had the money to consider capital projects – a hotel, an interactive rugby museum, a zip wire, a roofwalk – but it could not provide that basic job security for its elite players. Neither could it adequately fund the professional regions. Nor could it support the women's game. Nor, at that point, could it reform its own governance.

And so to the structure which underpins the national men's team.

Huw Richards, writing for ESPN nearly a decade ago, had a suggestion for the then newly-formed Professional Regional Game Board (PRGB): 'It needs to be asking what exactly the regional franchises are for? A decade after their creation we're no nearer an answer than when they were set up. Are they there purely to service the Welsh national team? If that is the case, they're not doing at all badly. But that also means that the focus of Welsh rugby – once a formidable social phenomenon – is essentially reduced to around a dozen games a year, of which only five are played in a competitive framework. That's a pretty narrow frame of reference, and scarcely sufficient to satisfy the real fan.'[9]

Eddie Butler agreed: 'The key to the success of regional rugby now is the fifth region – Wales, the national team. Wales have to play more, a minimum of 12 games per year, to finance the regions: more people watching more international rugby, generating more gate money than ever before. That is the contemporary equation. Rugby has become an upside-down game, nourished from above, not below. The regions, desperate for money, are losing more benefactors than they are acquiring... and they have become more dependent on the WRU cash injections as a result. The danger is that contact with the roots of the game has been lost. The top has become heavier and more important – some might argue more self-important – than the bottom of the game and it doesn't take a structural engineer to point out that such structures tend to come crashing down upon themselves.'[10]

The professional structure created in 2003 was neither one thing nor another. It did not contain only independent clubs as was the case in France and England, nor were they union-owned regional or provincial teams on the Ireland or New Zealand model. Some of them were mergers. Some of them took a financial hit to stand alone as, effectively, clubs. Debate has raged for all of the 20 years since their genesis. Should we go back to clubs? Should we restructure and create regional 'unions' which more closely resemble the currently successful Irish model? Should there be a professional team in north Wales, an area which had never produced a top-flight rugby team in the amateur era, nor during the period of national leagues?

These debates, while enervating/deeply tedious (delete as applicable) are rather moot. More important than how the teams are identified is the standard of rugby on offer. We have seen, after all, that Welsh crowds will turn out to support successful, competitive professional teams that are pushing for trophies. The great risk of the current financial reset is that it will ask supporters and sponsors – already struggling to maintain interest in the professional game – to keep on turning up and to keep on investing with little hope, never mind expectation, of success.

Either way, there now appears to be more clarity on the role of the professional teams. PRB now seem to be firmly of the view that four is the number of professional teams they want to see. All four are now in private ownership following the conclusion of an agreement for the WRU to relinquish its control of the Dragons and to put the club back into private hands for the first time since 2003.

The increasing gap between the professional and semi-professional tier is to be bridged, it is hoped, by a new competition – the Elite Domestic Competition (EDC) – which will sit between the professional and community game but will, crucially, fall under the remit of the Professional Rugby Board. Clubs will be invited to apply for time-limited franchises within firm parameters. There remains some scepticism among the clubs, but the new structure is expected to be launched in the 2024–25 season.

The professional teams are often criticised for not engaging their supporter base, of not being as attractive as the town clubs of the old structure. The argument doesn't stand up to analysis. Attendance figures for the pre-regional era are, for the most part, either unavailable or obviously flawed. Figures were not routinely published and, on the occasions that they were, usually ended in a suspiciously round number. For instance, in Celtic League rugby in 2001–02, Llanelli, Swansea and Cardiff all reported average attendances across the competition of precisely 4,000, while Pontypridd drew 3,200 and Ebbw Vale 2,000.[11] Even though attendances have fallen in the post-pandemic period, three of the professional teams attracted average crowds in excess of 7,000 in 2022–23, while the Dragons' average was just shy of 6,000 – figures far in excess of those drawn to the club structure of the late 1990s and early 2000s. A far cry from some of those great clashes of the 1970s, perhaps, but this is now a very different world.

If crowds aren't hitting the 8,000 or so initially demanded by David Moffett all those years ago, it is, perhaps, unsurprising. Welsh teams have been uncompetitive, and they've been playing in a domestic league which is, to put it politely, challenging for the supporter. All matches are now televised live, which means that games are played right across the weekend, from Friday evening to Sunday afternoon. There is no routine for the supporter of the type which existed during the club era. Neither are there – given that the URC now spans five countries across both hemispheres – away fans travelling in numbers in the way that supporters are able to in England and France.

Of greater importance, perhaps, is the absence of star players for much of the domestic season, as Michael Owen noted in an interview in the *Western Mail* in 2020: 'You have got 21 rounds of Pro14 matches during the season. How many of those are proper games? About eight weekends maybe, plus the play-offs. It's crap. That's not a competition that's going to sell. It's really not. It's pointless having Pro14 matches on international weekends. The competition is completely compromised when that happens. Why would you go and watch that? That's not a professional level competition when you are taking out the best players. You can dress it up however you want, but that's the truth. It's rubbish.'[12]

'What the French have realised,' adds Ron Jones, 'is that if you want a commercially attractive competition, you have to have something with its own life, its own momentum.'[13]

The economic crisis hitting the domestic tiers in Wales and England may yet force a cross-border league – featuring teams from both countries, among others – after 25 years of waiting. As the Rugby World Cup drew to a close, rumours emerged of English interest in a tie-in with the United Rugby Championship. While rather disingenuously referred to by the *Telegraph* as a British and Irish league with Italian and South African involvement – when what it clearly meant was a partnership or merger between the URC and the English Premiership – it was thought that parties on all sides were open to the idea. We have, of course, been here many, many times before.

And so, in late 2023, the game in Wales remains in a state of flux. A new independent board is taking shape, and a new chief executive, Abi Tierney, will shortly take up her position. A new Professional Rugby Agreement is taking effect which will significantly cut the budgets of the professional teams, and is sure to limit their competitiveness. A new semi-professional tier is, perhaps, on its way. The women's game is finally being taken more seriously, at least at Test level. And we await the findings of the Rafferty inquiry into the culture at the WRU.

If 2023 really is to see a significant and long-lasting reset in Welsh rugby, it will depend in large part on the structures which are now being put in place. As Huw Jones suggests: 'All of these things go back to the same old issues in terms of how you run an organisation. The first thing you do is you need the right structures and the right people in place. The basic governance. And until you've got the right people asking the right questions, things are not going to change. And that's going to be the challenge for them now. I think they now have the right structures, but they've got to have the right people in there who are going to challenge. Because if they don't have the right people, then having the right structures isn't going to get them very far at all.'[14]

Rugby may not have the all-encompassing hold on the Welsh sporting imagination that it once had, but it is still important. A good result – for our national team, yes, but for our region or club or school too – still has the power to put a spring in the step. Graham Henry, during his stint as national coach back in the 1990s, had understood the centrality of rugby to Welsh life, but was still amazed to open his bedroom curtains on the morning of his first Six Nations match in 1999 to see 20,000 Wales supporters in central Edinburgh. Nor had he quite grasped that 'the crowd would regard itself as part of the team',[15] kicking every ball and making every tackle with the XV on the pitch.

The sport still has the capacity to move, but it is struggling. In a relatively poor country, professionalism was always going to put a strain on the community-based nature of the game. For Welsh rugby to survive, let alone thrive, it must break the unhealthy habit of 140 years and unite, at all levels.

The difficulties of the past year could amount to no more than a pause before Wales disappears as a serious rugby nation. Or it could be the springboard from which we reset and revive. We don't have much time. If we are to survive and thrive, the nettle must be grasped. We have no alternative but to come together and to drive the game, not back to where it once was, but forward to where it should be.

There is no time like the present.

Endnotes

Introduction

1. Hobsbawm, E., *Nations and Nationalism since 1780* (Cambridge, 1990), p.143, quoted in Johnes, M., *A History of Sport in Wales* (Cardiff: University Of Wales Press, 2005), p.109.
2. Lile, B. and Farmer, D., 'The early development of association football in south Wales, 1890–1906', *Transactions of the Honourable Society of Cymmrodorion* (1984), pp.213–14, quoted in 'Irredeemably English? Football as a Welsh sport', *Planet*, 133, February–March 1999), pp.72–8.
3. George Ewart Evans, *The Strength of the Hills*, quoted in Williams, G., *1905 and all that* (Hyperion Books, 1991).
4. Williams, G., *1905 and all that* (Hyperion Books, 1991), p.86.
5. Jones, I.M., 'Win or lose today, Welsh football has shown rugby what a national sport looks like', 9/10/2017 [online]. Available at: https://nation.cymru/opinion/win-or-lose-today-welsh-football-has-shown-rugby-what-a-national-sport-looks-like/ [Accessed 23 October 2023].

Chapter 1: Decline and Fall

1. Smith, D. and Williams G., 'Beyond the Fields of Praise: Welsh Rugby 1980–1999', in Richards, H., Stead, P. and Williams, G., *More Heart and Soul* (1999), p.207.
2. Ibid.
3. Johnes, M., *A History of Sport in Wales* (University of Wales Press, 2005), p.82.
4. Smith, A., 'Civil war in England: The clubs, the RFU, and the impact of professionalism on Rugby Union, 1995–99', *Contemporary British History*, 14:2, p.149.
5. Slot, O., 'Lord of the ring masters', *The Independent*, 5/8/1995 [online]. Available at: https://www.independent.co.uk/sport/lord-of-the-ring-masters-1594991.html [Accessed 27 August 2023].
6. Davies, G., in conversation with the author, 2023.
7. Ibid.

8. Davies, J., *Rygbi Cymru – y Gêm yn y Gwaed*, S4C (2023).
9. Robertson, I., in Starmer-Smith, N. and Whitbread, *Whitbread Rugby World '89* (1988), p.118.
10. Davies, J., *Rygbi Cymru – y Gêm yn y Gwaed*, S4C (2023).
11. Smith, D. and Williams, G., 'Beyond the Fields of Praise: Welsh Rugby 1980–1999', in Richards, H., Stead, P. and Williams, G. (eds), *More Heart and Soul*, p.215.
12. Williams, G., *1905 and all that* (Hyperion Books, 1991), p.33.
13. Davies, J. and Corrigan, P., *Jonathan* (Arrow, 1989), p.173.
14. Morgan, K.O., *Rebirth of a Nation: Wales, 1880–1980*, p.349 in Johnes, M., *A History of Sport in Wales* (University of Wales Press, 2005, eBooks), p.102.
15. Billot, J., 'A Nation in Turmoil', in Jones, S., *Rothmans Rugby Union Yearbook, 1991–92* (20th ed., 1991), p.227.
16. Williams M., 'Breathing Fire into the Welsh Dragon', in Nigel Starmer-Smith and Robertson, I., *The Whitbread Rugby World '91* (1990), p.56.
17. Owen, A., *Welsh Brewers Ltd Rugby Annual for Wales 1991–92* (1991), p.26.
18. Smith, D. and Williams, G., 'Beyond the Fields of Praise: Welsh Rugby 1980–1999', in Richards, H., Stead, P. and Williams, G. (eds) *More Heart and Soul*, p.210.
19. Holmes, T., *My Life in Rugby* (1988), p.100.
20. Bishop, N. and Carter, A., *The Good, the Bad and the Ugly: The Rise and Fall of Pontypool RFC* (Random House, 2013), pp.178–9.
21. Smith, D. and Williams, G., 'Beyond the Fields of Praise: Welsh Rugby 1980' in Richards, H., Stead, P. and Williams, G., *More Heart and Soul*, p.210.
22. Owen, A., *Welsh Brewers Ltd Rugby Annual for Wales 1991–92* (1991), pp.2, 15.
23. Thomas, C., 'The Tribulations of Welsh Rugby', in Robertson, I. and Starmer-Smith, N., *The Whitbread Rugby World '94* (1993), p.40.
24. Hall, M., *The Mike Hall Story* (Y Lolfa, 2015), p.172.
25. Smith, D. and Williams, G., 'Beyond the Fields of Praise: Welsh Rugby 1980–1999' in Richards, H., Stead, P. and Williams, G. (eds) *More Heart and Soul*, p.212.
26. Hall, M., *The Mike Hall Story* (Y Lolfa, 2015), pp.153–7.
27. Thomas, C., 'The Tribulations of Welsh Rugby', in Robertson, I. and Starmer-Smith, N., *The Whitbread Rugby World '94* (1993), p.41.
28. Smith, A., 'Civil war in England: The clubs, the RFU, and

the impact of professionalism on rugby union, 1995–99',
Contemporary British History (2000), 14:2, p.150.

29. John, M., 'Chairman's programme notes', *Cardiff v Cross Keys Programme*, 3/1/1994.

30. Johnes, M., *A History of Sport in Wales* (University of Wales Press, 2005), p.82.

31. Smith, A., 'Civil war in England: The clubs, the RFU, and the impact of professionalism on Rugby Union, 1995–99', *Contemporary British History* (2000), 14:2, p.150.

32. Owen, A., *Welsh Brewers Ltd Rugby Annual for Wales 1996–7* (1996), p.2.

Chapter 2: An Open Game

1. Davies, T.G.R., *Rygbi Cymru – y Gêm yn y Gwaed*, S4C (2023).

2. Davies, G., in conversation with the author, 2023.

3. Jones, H., in conversation with the author, 2023.

4. Bishop, N. and Carter, A., *The Good, the Bad and the Ugly: The Rise and Fall of Pontypool RFC* (Random House, 2013), p.185.

5. Davies, G., in conversation with the author, 2023.

6. Hewett, C., 'Cabannes goes as Richmond sack 34', *The Independent*, 12/3/1999 [online]. Available at: https://www.independent.co.uk/sport/rugby-union-cabannes-goes-as-richmond-sack-34-1080052.html [Accessed 26 September 2023].

7. Jones, R., in conversation with the author, 2023.

8. *The Independent*, 'Rugby Union: WRU bails out troubled clubs', 24/1/1997 [online]. Available at: https://www.independent.co.uk/sport/rugby-union-wru-bails-out-troubled-clubs-1284874.html [Accessed 27 August 2023].

9. Rees, P., 'Player sues over contract', *The Irish Times*, 19/5/1998 [online]. Available at https://www.irishtimes.com/sport/player-sues-over-contract-1.154340 [Accessed 26 September 2023].

10. Davies, G., in conversation with the author, 2023.

11. Carter, A. and Bishop, N., *Seeing Red* (Random House, 2011), p.33.

12. Gough, I., *Goughy: A Tough Lock To Crack* (Y Lolfa, 2015), p.30.

13. Thomas, S., 'The sliding doors moment WRU turned down five places in Anglo-Welsh league to leave people stunned', WalesOnline, 26/6/2022 [online]. Available at: https://www.walesonline.co.uk/sport/rugby/rugby-news/sliding-doors-moment-wru-turned-24284725 [Accessed 27 August 2023].

14. news.bbc.co.uk, BBC News I Rugby Union, 'British League ruled

out this season', 18/8/1998 [online]. Available at: http://news.bbc. co.uk/1/hi/sport/rugby_union/153087.stm [Accessed 27 August 2023].

15. Davies, G., in conversation with the author, 2023.
16. Thomas, S., 'The sliding doors moment WRU turned down five places in Anglo-Welsh league to leave people stunned', WalesOnline. 26/6/2022 [online]. Available at: https://www. walesonline.co.uk/sport/rugby/rugby-news/sliding-doors-moment-wru-turned-24284725 [Accessed 27 August 2023].
17. Owen, A., *Rugby Annual for Wales 2000–2001* (2000), p.20.
18. Thomas, S., 'The sliding doors moment WRU turned down five places in Anglo-Welsh league to leave people stunned', WalesOnline. 26/6/2022 [online]. Available at: https://www. walesonline.co.uk/sport/rugby/rugby-news/sliding-doors-moment-wru-turned-24284725 [Accessed 27 August 2023].
19. Ibid.
20. Jones, R., in conversation with the author, 2023.
21. *Herald Scotland*, ' End of the line for new league', 3/2/1999 [online] Available at: https://www.heraldscotland.com/ news/12363018.end-of-the-line-for-new-league/ [Accessed 27 August 2023].
22. Thomas, S., 'The sliding doors moment WRU turned down five places in Anglo-Welsh league to leave people stunned', WalesOnline. 26/6/2022 [online]. Available at: https://www. walesonline.co.uk/sport/rugby/rugby-news/sliding-doors-moment-wru-turned-24284725 [Accessed 27 August 2023].
23. Glover, T., 'Rugby Union: Cardiff count cost of rebellion', *The Independent*, 24/4/1999 [online]. Available at: https://www. independent.co.uk/sport/rugby-union-cardiff-count-cost-of-rebellion-1089528.html [Accessed 27 August 2023].
24. Jones, H., 'Rugby Union: The Rebel Rousers; SWALEC Cup Final Special: Llanelli 10pts Swansea 37 – It was men against boys... going back to domestic Welsh rugby just doesn't interest us; says Scott Gibbs', *The Mirror*, Free Online Library, 17/5/1999 [online]. Available at: https://www.thefreelibrary.com/RUGBY+UNION%3 A+THE+REBEL+ROUSERS%3B+SWALEC+CUP+FINAL+SPEC IAL%3A+Llanelli...-a060385674 [Accessed 27 August 2023].

Chapter 3: Ruck the WRU

1. Howell, A., 'WRU EGM branded total farce by Llantwit Major chairman' (2023), Icwales, 27/5/2002 [online]. Available at:

https://web.archive.org/web/20030508204224/http:/icwales. icnetwork.co.uk/0500rugbyunion/0200news/page.cfm?objecti d=11904313&method=full&siteid=50082 [Accessed 27 August 2023].

2. Smith, D. and Williams, G., 'Beyond the Fields of Praise: Welsh Rugby 1980–1999', in Richards, H., Stead, P. and Williams, G. (eds), *More Heart and Soul* (1999), p.207.

3. Stewart, D., in Robertson, I. and Starmer-Smith, N., *Wooden Spoon Society Rugby World '01* (2000), p.130.

4. Jones, R., in conversation with the author, 2023.

5. Gough, I., *Goughy: A Tough Lock To Crack* (Y Lolfa, 2015), p.51.

6. Carter, A. and Bishop, N., *Seeing Red: Twelve Tumultuous Years in Welsh Rugby* (Random House, 2011), p.71.

7. Owen, A., *Buy As You View Rugby Annual for Wales 2001–2002* (2001), p.2 (Brown), p.3 (Pickering), p.57 (Thomas and Jenkins).

8. Gwladrugby, 'RPW Ltd statement', 8/10/2001 [online]. Available at: https://web.archive.org/web/20020622104058/http:/www. gwladrugby.com/clubs/misc/6Blueprint.htm [Accessed 27 August 2023].

9. Chow, T., 'Oz-truction', Gwladrugby, 23/11/2001 [online]. Available at: https://web.archive.org/web/20011214143420/http:// www.gwladrugby.com/clubhouse/newsarchive/November2001/ News231101.htm [Accessed 27 August 2023].

10. Gardiner, D., 'The Henry Blueprint for Success', *Match Programme, Cardiff v Swansea*, 9/1/1999.

11. Bishop, N. and Carter, A., *The Good, The Bad and The Ugly – The Rise and Fall of Pontypool RFC* (Random House, 2013), pp.198–9.

12. ESPN.com., '"Gang of six" present their plans to the WRU', 18/12/2001 [online]. Available at: https://www.espn.co.uk/rugby/ story/_/id/15359556/gang-six-present-their-plans-wru [Accessed 27 August 2023].

13. *South Wales Argus*, '"Welsh club rugby is bankrupt" – Gang of Six', 18/12/2001 [online]. Available at: https://www. southwalesargus.co.uk/news/6555271.welsh-club-rugby-is-bankrupt-gang-of-six/ [Accessed 27 August 2023].

14. Owen, A., *Buy As You View Rugby Annual for Wales 2002–2003* (2002).

15. BBC Sport Online, 'Edwards blasts WRU', 8/2/2002 [online]. Available at: http://news.bbc.co.uk/sport1/hi/rugby_union/ international/1808864.stm [Accessed 27 August 2023].

16. Chow, T., 'Feeling the heat', Gwladrugby, 7/2/2002 [online]. Available at: https://web.archive.org/web/20030116144512/http:/

www.gwladrugby.com/clubhouse/newsarchive/2002/February/
News070202.htm [Accessed 27 August 2023].

17. Blanche, P., Three Wales captains shocked at Henry's imminent
departure, 7/2/2002 [online]. Available at: https://web.archive.
org/web/20030508202852/http://icwales.icnetwork.co.uk/
0500rugbyunion/0200news/page.cfm?objectid=11597394&metho
d=full&siteid=50082 [Accessed 26 September 2023].

18. Carter, A. and Bishop, N., *Seeing Red: Twelve Tumultuous Years
in Welsh Rugby* (Random House, 2011), p74.

19. Keating, F., 'Henry's rise was unreal, his fall far more
predictable', *The Guardian*, 11/2/2002 [online]. Available at:
https://web.archive.org/web/20030118015614/http://sport.
guardian.co.uk/columnists/story/0,10260,648244,00.html
[Accessed 27 August 2023].

20. Rees, P., 'Welsh six angry at union's vote plan', *The Guardian*,
20/3/2002 [online]. Available at: https://www.theguardian.com/
sport/2002/mar/20/rugbyunion.sixnationsrugby20021 [Accessed
27 August 2023].

21. Owen, A., 'Tell WRU how to run the game', *Buy As You View
Rugby Annual for Wales 2000–2001* (2000), p.76.

22. Williams, R., 'Facing up to the future', Icwales,
21/2/2002 [online]. Available at: https://web.archive.
org/web/20030508203340/http://icwales.icnetwork.co.uk/
0500rugbyunion/0200news/page.cfm?objectid=11637713&metho
d=full&siteid=50082 [Accessed 27 August 2023].

23. Chow, T., 'Welsh Rugby: An Obituary', Gwladrugby.com,
25/3/2002 [online]. Available at: https://web.archive.org/
web/20030116145330/http:/www.gwladrugby.com/clubhouse/
newsarchive/2002/March/News250302.htm [Accessed 27 August
2023].

24. Griffiths, G., 'Calm Down, BT Deal Is Formality', *Welsh
Mirror*, 24/5/02 [online]. Available at: https://web.archive.
org/web/20021119174840/http://icscotland.icnetwork.co.uk/
news/mirror/today/page.cfm?objectid=11897029&method=full
[Accessed 27 August 2023].

25. Allsobrook, D., editor of Gwladrugby.com, in conversation with
the author, 2023.

26. Williams, B., 'Go Now: Welsh Mirror readers urge bungling
Welsh rugby chiefs to quit', *Welsh Mirror*, 3/4/2002 [online].
Available at: https://web.archive.org/web/20021121062947/http:/
icscotland.icnetwork.co.uk/news/mirror/today/page.cfm?objectid
=11755125&method=full [Accessed 27 August 2023].

27. Chow, T., 'Clubs will not be rushed into following anyone's agenda!', Gwladrugby, 5/4/2002 [online]. Available at: https:// web.archive.org/web/20020810163752/http://www.gwladrugby. com/clubhouse/newsarchive/2002/April/News050402.htm [Accessed 27 August 2023].

28. Williams, R., 'Welsh blazers playing politics as national team goes up in flames', *The Guardian*, 25/3/2002 [online]. Available at: https://web.archive.org/web/20030210071512/http://sport. guardian.co.uk/sixnations2002/story/0,11549,673347,00.html [Accessed 27 August 2023].

29. Owen, A., *Buy As You view Rugby Annual for Wales 2002–2003* (2002), pp.18–19.

30. Mason, T., 'What does the future hold for the WRU', *Western Mail*, 27/5/02 [online]. Available at: https://web.archive.org/ web/20030508211632/http:/icwales.icnetwork.co.uk/0100news/ 0100headlinesindex/page.cfm?objectid=11904257&method=full &siteid=50082 [Accessed 27 August 2023].

31. *South Wales Argus*, 'What a load of rubbish that was', 28/5/2002 [online]. Available at: https://www.southwalesargus.co.uk/ news/6555079.what-a-load-of-rubbish-that-was/ [Accessed 27 August 2023].

32. Howell, A., 'WRU EGM branded total farce by Llantwit Major chairman', *Western Mail*, 27/5/2002 [online]. Available at: https:// web.archive.org/web/20030508204224/http://icwales.icnetwork. co.uk/0500rugbyunion/0200news/page.cfm?objectid=11904313& method=full&siteid=50082 [Accessed 27 August 2023].

33. Owen, A., *Buy As You view Rugby Annual for Wales 2002–2003* (2002), p.2.

34. Davies, T.G.R., in Chow T., 'Welsh Rugby (1881–2002): An Obituary', Gwladrugby, 25/3/2002 [online]. Available at: https:// web.archive.org/web/20030116145330/http:/www.gwladrugby. com/clubhouse/newsarchive/2002/March/News250302.htm [Accessed 27 August 2023].

Chapter 4: Rise of the Regionalists

1. Davies, T.G.R., 'After years of neglect, the game is almost up for sorry Wales', www.thetimes.co.uk., 21/2/2003 [online]. Available at: https://www.thetimes.co.uk/article/after-years-of-neglect-the-game-is-almost-up-for-sorry-wales-9wznld3fl98 [Accessed 27 August 2023].

2. King, J., 'Swansea backers close to pulling the plug', *Western*

Mail, 4/6/2002 [online]. Available at: https://web.archive. org/web/20021130160143/http://icwales.icnetwork.co.uk/ 0500rugbyunion/0200news/page.cfm?objectid=11924291&metho d=full&siteid=50082 [Accessed 27 August 2023].

3. Williams, B. and Lamport, J., 'It's the last chance saloon; Exclusive Special Report: What Now For Welsh Rugby? Hung-Over WRU Has No Head For Modern Game', *Welsh Mirror*, 30/3/2002 [online]. Available at: https://www.thefreelibrary.com/ It%27s+the+last+chance+saloon%3B+EXCLUSIVE+SPECIAL+ REPORT%3A+WHAT+NOW+FOR...-a084279499 [Accessed 27 August 2023].

4. Howell, A., 'WRU looks to in-house overseers', *Western Mail*, 14/6/2002 [online]. Available at: https://web.archive. org/web/20020821081745/http:/icwales.icnetwork.co.uk/ 0500rugbyunion/0200news/page.cfm?objectid=11950318&metho d=full [Accessed 27 August 2023].

5. Lewis, Rh., 'Wizards lose promotion poll', Gwladrugby, 21/7/2002 [online]. Available at: https://web.archive.org/ web/20030116143718/http://www.gwladrugby.com/clubhouse/ newsarchive/2002/July/News210702.htm [Accessed 27 August 2023].

6. *Western Mail*, 'Glanmor survives new calls to quit', 21/7/2002 [online]. Available at: https://web.archive. org/web/20020811062832/http://icwales.icnetwork.co.uk/ 0500rugbyunion/0200news/page.cfm?objectid=12052228&metho d=full&siteid=50082 [Accessed 27 August 2023].

7. Jones, A., 'Crisis? What Crisis?', Gwladrugby, 22/7/2002 [online]. Available at: https://web.archive.org/web/20030116144321/ http://www.gwladrugby.com/clubhouse/newsarchive/2002/July/ News220702.htm [Accessed 27 August 2023].

8. Rees, P., 'WRU feels the pinch as Barclays oversees cutback', *The Guardian*, 4/7/2002 [online]. Available at: https://web.archive.org/ web/20030119150314/http://sport.guardian.co.uk/rugbyunion/ story/0,10069,748874,00.html [Accessed 27 August 2023].

9. Williams, P., 'Wales stars face pay cut', *Daily Mirror*, 4/7/2002 [online]. Available at: https://web.archive. org/web/20020811052641/http:/icwales.icnetwork.co.uk/ 0500rugbyunion/0200news/page.cfm?objectid=12006008&metho d=full&siteid=50082 [Accessed 27 August 2023].

10. Rees, P., 'WRU feels the pinch as Barclays Bank oversees cutbacks', *The Guardian*, 4/7/2002 [online]. Available at: https:// web.archive.org/web/20030119150314/http://sport.guardian.

co.uk/rugbyunion/story/0,10069,748874,00.html [Accessed 27 August 2023].

11. Howell, A., 'Porthcawl tells Samuel to "mind his own"', *Western Mail*, 17/7/2002 [online]. Available at: https://web.archive. org/web/20030508202246/http://icwales.icnetwork.co.uk/ 0500rugbyunion/0200news/page.cfm?objectid=12036571&metho d=full&siteid=50082 [Accessed 27 August 2023].

12. Roberts, G., 'Vale of tears for the Steelmen', *Western Mail*, 19/7/2002 [online]. Available at: https://web.archive. org/web/20030508202558/http://icwales.icnetwork.co.uk/ 0500rugbyunion/0200news/page.cfm?objectid=12045688&metho d=full&siteid=50082 [Accessed 27 August 2023].

13. Roberts, G., 'Pritchard quits Caerphilly', *Western Mail*, 26/7/2002 [online]. Available at: https://web.archive.org/ web/20030314062452/http://news.bbc.co.uk/sport1/hi/rugby_ union/celtic/2151513.stm [Accessed 27 August 2023].

14. Rees, P., 'Stalemate over Woodward plan', *The Guardian*, 8/8/2002 [online]. Available at: https://web.archive.org/ web/20020817211405/http:/sport.guardian.co.uk/rugbyunion/ story/0,10069,770984,00.html [Accessed 27 August 2023].

15. Sporting Wales, 'Welsh Players in comfort zone', 3/9/2002 [online]. Available at: https://web.archive.org/ web/20030120164335/http:/www.sportingwales.com/artman/ publish/article_1925.shtml [Accessed 27 August 2023].

16. Roberts, G., 'Huge disparity between the Premier clubs', *Western Mail*, 4/9/2002 [online]. Available at: https://web.archive. org/web/20021128181913/http://icwales.icnetwork.co.uk/ 0500rugbyunion/0200news/page.cfm?objectid=12169693&metho d=full&siteid=50082 [Accessed 27 August 2023].

17. Howell, A., 'Ruddock calls for two-tier funding plan', *Western Mail*, 5/9/2002 [online]. Available at: https://web.archive. org/web/20021128182052/http://icwales.icnetwork.co.uk/ 0500rugbyunion/0200news/page.cfm?objectid=12172758&metho d=full&siteid=50082 [Accessed 27 August 2023].

18. Howell, A., 'Samuel so angry at fans' outburst', *Western Mail*, 5/9/2002 [online]. Available at: https://web.archive. org/web/20021128181944/http://icwales.icnetwork.co.uk/ 0500rugbyunion/0200news/page.cfm?objectid=12172764&metho d=full&siteid=50082 [Accessed 27 August 2023].

19. Baker, G., 'Will not pay players, says Bull', *South Wales Argus*, 7/10/2002 [online]. Available at: https://web.archive. org/web/20021224202242/http://www.thisisgwent.co.uk/gwent/

archive/2002/10/07/sport1033991469ZM.html [Accessed 27 August 2023].

20. Jones, G., 'Clubs at grass roots counting cost of the stampede for money since game went open', *Western Mail*, 4/10/2002 [online]. Available at: https://web.archive.org/web/20021128180814/ http://icwales.icnetwork.co.uk/0500rugbyunion/0200news/page. cfm?objectid=12252904&method=full&siteid=50082 [Accessed 27 August 2023].

21. *Western Mail*, 'Numbers mask serious problem', *Western Mail*, 30/10/2002 [online]. Available at: https://web.archive. org/web/20021224220624/http:/icwales.icnetwork.co.uk/ 0500rugbyunion/0200news/page.cfm?objectid=12322571&metho d=full&siteid=50082 [Accessed 27 August 2023].

22. Johnes, M., *A History of Sport in Wales* (University of Wales Press eBooks, 2005), p.105, taken from Sports Council of Wales, *Sports Participation and Club Membership in Wales 1998/99*, pp.9–10.

23. Moffett, D., in conversation with the author, 2023.

24. Blyth, R. (2013) in Owen, P., *10 Years of the Ospreys* (Y Lolfa, 2014), p.5.

25. *South Wales Argus*, 'Superclubs plan scuppered', 9/12/2002 [online]. Available at: https://www.southwalesargus.co.uk/ news/6554995.superclubs-plan-scuppered/ [Accessed 27 August 2023].

26. Thomas, S., 'Fears over four-team plan for Welsh rugby', *South Wales Echo*, 25/10/2002 [online]. Available at: https://www. thefreelibrary.com/Rugby+Union%3A+Fears+over+four-team+pl an+for+Welsh+rugby.-a093436584 [Accessed 27 August 2023].

27. Jones, S., 'Welsh rugby on its knees', *Sunday Times*, 27/10/2002 [online]. Available at: https://www.thetimes.co.uk/article/welsh-rugby-on-its-knees-sfr332m3gvx [Accessed 27 August 2023].

28. Williams, S., 'Farewell to a legend', Gwladrugby, 4/10/2002 [online]. Available at: https://web.archive.org/ web/20021208080732/http://www.gwladrugby.com/clubhouse/ newsarchive/2002/October/News041002.htm [Accessed 27 August 2023].

29. Jones, S., 'Welsh rugby on its knees', *Sunday Times*, 27/10/2002 [online]. Available at: https://www.thetimes.co.uk/article/welsh-rugby-on-its-knees-sfr332m3gvx [Accessed 27 August 2023].

30. BBC Sport Online, 'Bridgend and Neath form alliance', 3/12/2002 [online]. Available at: http://news.bbc.co.uk/sport1/hi/rugby_ union/celtic/2540959.stm [Accessed 26 September 2023].

31. Stephens, H., 'Moffett's Mix'n'match: Clubs staggered by plans

for four regions', *The Mirror*, 6/12/2002 [online]. Available at: https://www.thefreelibrary.com/RUGBY+UNION%3A+MOFFET T'S+MIX+'N+MATCH%3B+Clubs+staggered+by+plan+for+four.. .-a094967579 [Accessed 27 August 2023].

32. Bishop, N. and Carter, A., *The Good, The Bad and The Ugly – The Rise and Fall of Pontypool RFC* (2014), p.201.

33. BBC Sport Online, 'Merger plan sparks angry reaction', 4/12/2002 [online]. Available at: http://news.bbc.co.uk/sport1/hi/ rugby_union/celtic/2541937.stm [Accessed 27 August 2023].

34. BBC Sport Online, 'Clubs reject Moffett's proposal', 10/12/2002 [online]. Available at: http://news.bbc.co.uk/sport1/hi/rugby_ union/celtic/2560953.stm [Accessed 27 August 2023].

35. BBC Sport Online, 'Welsh clubs "close to a compromise"', 12/12/2002 [online]. Available at: http://news.bbc.co.uk/sport1/hi/ rugby_union/celtic/2587741.stm [Accessed 27 August 2023].

36. Thomas, S., 'Valleys must not miss out like our friends in the north', *South Wales Echo*, 9/1/2003 [online]. Available at: https:// www.thefreelibrary.com/Rugby+Union%3A+Valleys+must+no t+miss+out+like+our+friends+in+north%3B+At...-a096299308 [Accessed 27 August 2023].

37. BBC Sport Online, 'Moffett scraps northern expansion', 8/1/2003 [online]. Available at: http://news.bbc.co.uk/sport1/hi/rugby_ union/celtic/2639325.stm [Accessed 27 August 2023].

38. Howells, L., *Despite the Knock-backs – The Autobiography of Lynn Howells* (Y Lolfa, 2013, Kindle Edition), Location 307.

39. BBC Sport Online, 'Independence costs Llanelli', 22/1/2003 [online]. Available at: http://news.bbc.co.uk/sport1/hi/rugby_ union/celtic/2685237.stm [Accessed 27 August 2023].

40. BBC Sport Online, 'Four franchises for the future', 23/1/2003 [online]. Available at: http://news.bbc.co.uk/sport1/hi/rugby_ union/celtic/2689475.stm [Accessed 27 August 2023].

41. BBC Sport Online, 'Clubs react to regional plan', 24/01/2003 [online]. Available at: http://news.bbc.co.uk/sport1/hi/ wales/2690879.stm [Accessed 27 August 2023].

42. BBC Sport, 'Ponty merger angers Samuel', 25/01/2003 [online]. Available at: http://news.bbc.co.uk/sport1/hi/rugby_union/ celtic/2705057.stm [Accessed 27 August 2023].

43. Howells, L., *Despite the Knock-backs – The Autobiography of Lynn Howells* (Y Lolfa, 2013, Kindle Edition), Location 307.

44. BBC Sport Online, 'Llanelli remain last regional hurdle', 20/2/2003 [online]. Available at: http://news.bbc.co.uk/sport1/hi/ rugby_union/celtic/2709411.stm [Accessed 27 August 2023].

45. Thomas, S., 'Moffett keeps cards close to his chest', *South Wales Echo*, 12/2/2003 [online]. Available at: https://www.thefreelibrary. com/Rugby+Union%3a+Moffett+keeps+cards+close+to+his+ches t.-a097514548 [Accessed 27 August 2023].

46. Rees, P., 'Llanelli's legal move forces five-club line', *The Guardian*, 20/3/2003 [online]. Available at: https://www. theguardian.com/sport/2003/mar/20/rugbyunion.llanelliscarlets [Accessed 27 August 2023].

47. Gallagher, B., 'Llanelli take WRU to court', *The Telegraph*, 20/3/2003 [online]. Available at: https://www.telegraph.co.uk/ sport/rugbyunion/international/wales/2398316/Llanelli-take-WRU-to-court.html [Accessed 27 August 2023].

48. Jones, R., in conversation with the author, 2023.

49. Jones, S., 'WRU move in right direction', *Sunday Times*, 23/3/2003 [online]. Available at: https://www.thetimes.co.uk/ article/stephen-jones-wru-move-in-right-direction-6x2bm83c6lf [Accessed 27 August 2023].

50. Wales Online, '£2.5m: Swansea's debt revealed', 9/5/2003 [online]. Available at: https://www.walesonline.co.uk/sport/rugby/ rugby-news/25m-swanseas-debt-revealed-2484122 [Accessed 27 August 2023].

51. Billot, J., 'Domestic Rugby in Wales 2002–03', in Griffiths, J. and Cleary, M., *IRB International Rugby Yearbook 2003–2004* (2003), p.450.

52. Tolley, C. and Currie, M., 'Victim of rugby's new era: Griffiths is casualty of Moffett's regime, says legend Bennett', *Daily Post*, 7/6/2003 [online]. Available at: https://www.thefreelibrary.com/ Rugby+union%3a+Victim+of+rugby%27s+new+era%3b+Griffith s+is+casualty+of...-a0102942578 [Accessed 27 August 2023].

53. Scott, J., 'Out with the old and in with the not-so-new', 9/6/2003 [online]. Available at: https://www.thefreelibrary.com/Rugby+ Union%3a+Out+with+the+old+and+in+with+the+not-so+new.-a0102926198 [Accessed 27 August 2023].

54. Moffett, D., in conversation with the author, 2023.

Chapter 5: A New Year Nearing, Full of Relentless Surprises

1. Moffett, D., in conversation with the author, 2023.

2. Thomas, G. and Calvin, M., *Proud* (Ebury Press, 2015), p.87.

3. Gibson, J., 'More hated than Osama bin Laden', *Newcastle Evening Chronicle*, 7/9/2004 [online]. Available at: https://www.

thefreelibrary.com/More+hated+than+Osama+bin+Laden.-a0121669871 [Accessed 27 August 2023].

4. Billot, J., 'Wales Test Season Review 2002–2003', *International Rugby Yearbook 2003–2004* (2003), p.208.

5. Carter, A. and Bishop, N., *Seeing Red – Twelve Tumultuous Years in Welsh Rugby* (Random House, 2011), p.122.

6. Howells, L., *Despite the Knock-backs – The Autobiography of Lynn Howells* (Y Lolfa, 2013, Kindle Edition), Location 262.

7. BBC News, 'Newport win Dragons fight', 21/8/2003 [online]. Available at: http://news.bbc.co.uk/sport1/hi/rugby_union/welsh/3171467.stm [Accessed 28 August 2023].

8. Welsh Rugby Union | Wales & Regions, 'Pontypridd Go Into Administration', 23/9/2003 [online]. Available at: https://www.wru.wales/2003/09/pontypridd-go-into-administration/ [Accessed 28 August 2023].

9. Rees, P., 'Bridgend wag the Warriors as Pontypridd go under', *The Guardian*, 27/9/2003 [online]. Available at: https://www.theguardian.com/sport/2003/sep/27/rugbyunion.paulrees [Accessed 28 August 2023].

10. Howells, L., *Despite the Knock-backs – The Autobiography of Lynn Howells* (Y Lolfa, 2013, Kindle Edition), Location 883.

11. Jones, A., 'Samuel Peeps', Gwladrugby, 7/4/2003 [online]. Available at: https://web.archive.org/web/20040607004519/http://www.gwladrugby.com/Clubhouse/NewsArchive/Date.php?News=57 [Accessed 28 August 2023].

12. Howells, L., *Despite the Knock-backs – The Autobiography of Lynn Howells* (Y Lolfa, 2013, Kindle Edition), Location 213.

13. Davies, S., 'Valleys wasteland envisaged', BBC Sport, 19/5/2004 [online]. Available at: http://news.bbc.co.uk/sport1/hi/rugby_union/welsh/3728307.stm [Accessed 28 August 2023].

14. BBC Sport, 'WRU axe falls on Warriors', 1/6/2004 [online]. Available at: http://news.bbc.co.uk/sport1/hi/rugby_union/welsh/3754959.stm [Accessed 28 August 2023].

15. Thomas, G. and Calvin, M., *Proud* (Ebury Press, 2015), p.111.

16. Howell, A., 'The inside story of the Welsh rugby team that disappeared, 16 years on from the bitter collapse of the Celtic Warriors', Wales Online, 20/1/2019 [online]. Available at: https://www.walesonline.co.uk/sport/rugby/rugby-news/inside-story-welsh-rugby-team-15679375 [Accessed 28 August 2023].

17. Jones, R., in conversation with the author, 2023.

18. Howell, A., 'The inside story of the Welsh rugby team that disappeared, 16 years on from the bitter collapse of the Celtic

Warriors', *Wales Online*, 20/1/2019 [online]. Available at: https://www.walesonline.co.uk/sport/rugby/rugby-news/inside-story-welsh-rugby-team-15679375 [Accessed 28 August 2023].

19. Cobner, T., 'My Story', 30/7/2004 [online]. Available at: https://www.walesonline.co.uk/sport/rugby/rugby-news/terry-cobner-my-story-2431655 [Accessed 28 August 2023].

20. Carter, A. and Bishop, N., *Seeing Red: Twelve Tumultuous Years in Welsh Rugby* (Random House, 2011), p.119.

21. Owen, P., *10 Years of the Ospreys* (Y Lolfa, 2014), p.55.

22. Lowe, A., '"Celtic Rugby is dying" – Moffett: WRU Chief issues a warning', 28/11/2005 [online]. Available at: https://www.thefreelibrary.com/RUGBY+UNION+Celtic+rugby+is+dying+-+Moffett%3b+WRU+chief+issues+a...-a0139161212 [Accessed 28 August 2023].

23. Wishart, C., 'Wales says goodbye to Grand Slam hero: But visionary Moffett leaves a legacy at the WRU', *Daily Post*, 30/9/2005 [online]. Available at: https://www.thefreelibrary.com/Rugby+Union%3a+Wales+says+goodbye+to+Grand+Slam+hero%3b+But+visionary...-a0136872258 [Accessed 28 August 2023].

24. Howells, L., *Despite the Knock-backs – The Autobiography of Lynn Howells* (Y Lolfa, 2013, Kindle Edition), Location 156.

25. Moffett, D., in conversation with the author, 2023.

26. Jones, H., in conversation with the author, 2023.

27. Byrne, L. *The Byrne Identity* (Y Lolfa, 2017), p.46.

28. Carter, A. and Bishop, N., *Seeing Red: Twelve Tumultuous Years in Welsh Rugby* (Random House, 2011), p.172.

29. Jones, A., *Bomb* (Headline, 2015, Kindle edition), Location 1877.

30. Thomas, G. and Calvin, M., *Proud* (Ebury Press, 2015), p.149.

31. Carter, A. and Bishop, N., *Seeing Red: Twelve Tumultuous Years in Welsh Rugby* (Random House, 2011), p.177.

32. Ibid.

33. Thomas, G. and Calvin, M., *Proud* (Ebury Press, 2015), p.149.

34. Gough, I., *Goughy: A Tough Lock To Crack* (Y Lolfa, 2015), p.79.

35. Jones, R., in conversation with the author, 2023.

36. Rees, P., 'Celtic League ejects Welsh clubs', *The Guardian*, 31/5/2005 [online]. Available at: https://www.theguardian.com/sport/2005/jun/01/rugbyunion.llanelliscarlets [Accessed 28 August 2023].

37. Welsh Rugby Union I Wales & Regions, 'Celtic League Solution Found', 17/6/2005 [online]. Available at: https://www.wru.wales/2005/06/celtic-league-solution-found/ [Accessed 28 August 2023].

38. Byrne, L., *The Byrne Identity* (Y Lolfa, 2017), pp.39–40.
39. North Wales Live, 'Jenkins stands firm at Twickers debacle', 7/8/2007 [online]. Available at: https://www.dailypost.co.uk/ sport/rugby-union/jenkins-stands-firm-twickers-debacle-2867258 [Accessed 28 August 2023].
40. Lea, R., 'Roger Lewis, the Welsh Rugby Union boss, has the ball at his feet', *The Times*, 16/3/2013 [online]. Available at: https:// www.thetimes.co.uk/article/roger-lewis-the-welsh-rugby-union-boss-has-the-ball-at-his-feet-sqsskrbpln0?gclid=CjwKCAjwkLCkB hA9EiwAka9QRg7Dmxks0CAPVL7Z2zb5j0zo0lIo4WSTrSJBPxvg sZfvFyxVva5eABoCx5kQAvD_BwE [Accessed 28 August 2023].
41. Jones, A., *Bomb* (Headline, 2015, Kindle edition), Location 2357.
42. Gough, I., *Goughy: A Tough Lock To Crack* (Y Lolfa, 2015), p.91.

Chapter 6: The Most Powerful Man in Rock

1. Butler, E., 'Wales regions' chorus of anger finds voice against WRU's Roger Lewis', *The Guardian*, 6/4/2013 [online]. Available at: https://www.theguardian.com/sport/blog/2013/apr/06/wales-regions-wru-george-north [Accessed 28 August 2023].
2. Woodrow, E., 'Roger Lewis: from music boss to rugby supremo', Wales Online, 1/9/2012 [online]. Available at: https://www. walesonline.co.uk/lifestyle/showbiz/roger-lewis-music-boss-rugby-2023342 [Accessed 28 August 2023].
3. Gatland, W., *Pride and Passion* (Headline, 2019), p.153.
4. ESPN Rugby, 'WRU and Regions map out the future', 30/1/2008 [online]. Available at: https://www.espn.co.uk/rugby/story/_/ id/15404826/wru-regions-map-future [Accessed 28 August 2023].
5. Rees, P., 'Moffett to blame for Welsh rugby's latest split', *The Guardian*, 21/10/2008 [online]. Available at: https://www. theguardian.com/sport/blog/2008/oct/28/walesrugbyunionteam-magnersleague [Accessed 28 August 2023].
6. Moffett, D., in conversation with the author, 2023.
7. WRU, 'WRU and regions agree new five-year deal', 8/9/2009 [online]. Available at: https://community.wru.wales/2009/09/08/ wru-and-regions-agree-new-five-year-deal/ [Accessed 28 August 2023].
8. BBC Sport, 'WRU take control of North Wales regional team', 20/1/2011 [online]. Available at: http://news.bbc.co.uk/sport1/hi/ rugby_union/welsh/9368239.stm [Accessed 28 August 2023].
9. BBC Sport, 'Gareth Davies calls for action over poor regional attendances', 7/12/2011 [online]. Available at: https://www.bbc.

co.uk/sport/rugby-union/16055602 [Accessed 28 August 2023].

10. BBC Sport, 'Wales player exits alarms Scarlets coach Nigel Davies', 7/12/2011 [online]. Available at: https://www.bbc.co.uk/sport/rugby-union/16059201 [Accessed 28 August 2023].

11. Bishop, N. and Carter, A., *The Good, The Bad and The Ugly – The Rise and Fall of Pontypool RFC* (Random House, 2013), p.216.

12. Roberts, J. and Harries, R., *Centre Stage* (Hachette UK, 2021), p.226.

13. Byrne, L., *The Byrne Identity* (Y Lolfa, 2017), p.64.

14. BBC Sport, 'Damning report questions survival of Welsh rugby regions', 7/11/2012 [online]. Available at: https://www.bbc.co.uk/sport/rugby-union/20218179 [Accessed 28 August 2023].

15. Hewett, C., 'Roger Lewis: "French clubs are endangering the European game"', 3/11/2012 [online]. Available at: https://www.independent.co.uk/sport/rugby/rugby-union/club-rugby/roger-lewis-french-clubs-are-endangering-the-european-game-8277961.html [Accessed 28 August 2023].

16. Bishop, N. and Carter, A., *The Good, The Bad and The Ugly – The Rise and Fall of Pontypool RFC* (Random House, 2013), p.219.

17. Ospreysrugby.com, 'Statement from Regional Rugby Wales', 7/2/2013 [online]. Available at: https://www.ospreysrugby.com/news/statement-regional-rugby-wales-4 [Accessed 28 August 2023].

18. North Wales Live, 'WRU accuse Scarlets over George North transfer talks', 31/3/2013 [online]. Available at: https://www.dailypost.co.uk/sport/rugby-union/wru-accuse-scarlets-over-george-2638055 [Accessed 28 August 2023].

19. Author unknown, 'Statement On Behalf Of The 4 Welsh Rugby Regions', *West Wales Chronicle*, 2/4/2013 [online]. Available at: https://www.westwaleschronicle.co.uk/blog/2013/04/02/statement-on-behalf-of-the-4-welsh-rugby-regions/ [Accessed 28 August 2023].

20. Gwladrugby, 'Everything you wanted to know about Welsh rugby, but were afraid to ask', 4/1/2014 [online]. Available at: https://gwladrugby.wordpress.com/2014/01/04/everything-you-wanted-to-know-about-welsh-rugby-but-were-afraid-to-ask/ [Accessed 28 August 2023].

Chapter 7: One for You, Two for Me

1. BBC Sport, 'Lewis' warning for Welsh regions', 6/10/2013 [online] Available at: https://www.bbc.co.uk/sport/rugby-union/24412491 [Accessed 28 August 2023].

2. Jones, B., in conversation with the author, 2023.
3. Gwladrugby, 'Minutes of the Joint Supporters Group meeting with the Welsh Rugby Union, 16th December 2013', 8/1/2014 [online] Available at: https://gwladrugby.wordpress.com/2014/01/08/minutes-of-the-joint-supporters-group-meeting-with-the-welsh-rugby-union-16th-december-2013/ [Accessed 28 August 2023].
4. Hewett, C., 'Roger Lewis: "French clubs are endangering the European game"', *The Independent*, 3/11/2012 [online]. Available at: https://www.independent.co.uk/sport/rugby/rugby-union/club-rugby/roger-lewis-french-clubs-are-endangering-the-european-game-8277961.html [Accessed 28 August 2023].
5. Ibid.
6. Butler, E., 'Wales regions' chorus of anger finds voice against WRU's Roger Lewis', *The Guardian*, 6/4/2013 [online]. Available at: https://www.theguardian.com/sport/blog/2013/apr/06/wales-regions-wru-george-north [Accessed 28 August 2023].
7. Gwladrugby, 'Minutes of the Joint Supporters Group meeting with Regional Rugby Wales, Sunday 22nd December 2013', 8/1/2014 [online]. Available at: https://gwladrugby.wordpress.com/2014/01/08/minutes-of-the-joint-supporters-group-meeting-with-regional-rugby-wales-sunday-22nd-december-2013/ [Accessed 28 August 2023].
8. ESPN, 'Welsh regions offered £4m to join Premiership', 29/12/2013 [online] Available at: http://en.espn.co.uk/wales/rugby/story/209805.html [Accessed 28 August 2023].
9. ESPN, 'D-Day looms for Welsh rugby', 31/12/2013 [online]. Available at: http://en.espn.co.uk/wales/rugby/story/209917.html [Accessed 28 August 2023].
10. ESPN Scrum, 'Wales Rugby: WRU will not allow regions to join Champions Cup', 4/1/2014 [online]. Available at: http://en.espn.co.uk/wales/rugby/story/210149.html [Accessed 28 August 2023].
11. ESPN Scrum, 'Wales: WRU to move top stars to England?', 5/1/2014 [online]. Available at: http://en.espn.co.uk/wales/rugby/story/210227.html [Accessed 28 August 2023].
12. Alastair Eykyn, BBC Radio 5 Live, 12/1/2014 [online]. Available at: https://www.youtube.com/watch?v=Il5Zj4CmptQ [Accessed 28 August 2023].
13. Moffett, D., in conversation with the author, 2023.
14. Allsobrook, D., in conversation with the author, 2023.
15. ITV Wales News, 'WRU Chief: Regional row has left world rugby "bemused"', 21/1/2014 [online]. Available at: https://www.itv.com/

news/wales/2014-01-21/wru-chief-regional-row-has-left-world-rugby-bemused [Accessed 28 August 2023].

16. Gwladrugby, 'One Big Lie', 21/1/2014 [online]. Available at: https://gwladrugby.wordpress.com/2014/01/21/one-big-lie/ [Accessed 28 August 2023].

17. Gwladrugby, 'Robert Davies Lets Rip at Roger', 5/2/2014 [online] Available at: https://gwladrugby.wordpress.com/2014/02/05/robert-davies-lets-rip-at-roger/ [Accessed 27 August 2023].

18. BBC Wales, 'Welsh regions "lack trust" in Welsh Rugby Union', 28/2/2014 [online] Available at: https://www.bbc.co.uk/sport/rugby-union/26393735 [Accessed 28 August 2023].

19. Moffett, D., in conversation with the author, 2023.

20. Moffett, D., '"Moffesto" launched: former CEO lays out his agenda for change', Gwladrugby, 28/3/2014 [online]. Available at: https://gwladrugby.wordpress.com/2014/03/28/moffesto-launched-former-ceo-lays-out-his-agenda-for-change/ [Accessed 28 August 2023].

21. Moffett, D., in conversation with the author, 2023.

22. Taylor, J., ESPN Scrum, 'A very unfunny Welsh farce', 18/6/2014 [online]. Available at: http://en.espn.co.uk/blogs/rugby/story/230201.html [Accessed 28 August 2023].

23. Howell, A., 'How David Moffett's crusade against the WRU came to an end at the Extraordinary General Meeting', Wales Online, 16/6/2014 [online]. Available at: https://www.walesonline.co.uk/sport/rugby/rugby-news/andy-howell-how-after-shock-7271515?int_source=amp_continue_reading&int_medium=amp&int_campaign=continue_reading_button#amp-readmore-target [Accessed 28 August 2023].

24. ESPN Staff, 'Gloves off as hopes of Welsh deal collapse', ESPN Rugby, 11/7/2014 [online]. Available at: http://en.espn.co.uk/wales/rugby/story/233581.html [Accessed 28 August 2023].

25. Turner, P., 'A dignified, listening Union?', Gwladrugby, 22/9/2014 [online]. Available at: https://gwladrugby.wordpress.com/2014/09/22/a-dignified-listening-union/ [Accessed 28 August 2023].

26. Gwladrugby, 'More WRU spin... so who do you believe?', 9/9/2014 [online]. Available at: https://gwladrugby.wordpress.com/2014/09/09/more-wru-spin-so-who-do-you-believe/ [Accessed 28 August 2023].

27. Davies, G., in conversation with the author, 2023.

28. Ibid.

29. Jeffreys, B., 'The power of collaboration – a new era for Welsh

rugby awaits', Gwladrugby, 31/10/2015 [online]. Available at: https://gwladrugby.wordpress.com/2015/10/31/the-power-of-collaboration-a-new-era-for-welsh-rugby-awaits/ [Accessed 28 August 2023].

Chapter 8: Partnership, Reset

1. Rees, P., 'Welsh regions still playing catch-up with Irish despite Scarlets' success', *The Guardian*, 19/4/2018 [online]. Available at: https://www.theguardian.com/sport/2018/apr/19/breakdown-ireland-provinces-wales-regions-scarlets-leinster [Accessed 27/9/2023].
2. Byrne, L., *The Byrne Identity* (Y Lolfa, 2017), p.59.
3. Williams, S., 'Final day meltdown was just not acceptable', *The Rugby Paper*, 13/5/2016 [online]. Available at: https://www.therugbypaper.co.uk/all/columnists/shane-williams/25863/shane-williams-column-final-day-meltdown-was-just-not-acceptable/ [Accessed 28 August 2023].
4. BBC Sport, 'Welsh rugby: Review called, but no crisis says Gareth Davies', 11/5/2016 [online]. Available at: https://www.bbc.co.uk/sport/rugby-union/36266158 [Accessed 28 August 2023].
5. WRU, 'Our Strategy for Welsh Rugby', 3/11/2016 [online]. Available at: https://www.wru.wales/2016/11/our-strategy-for-welsh-rugby/ [Accessed 28 August 2023].
6. Davies, G., in conversation with the author, 2023.
7. Thomas, S., '"We are heading for a car crash in regional rugby", The stark message from Cardiff Blues chairman Peter Thomas', 3/1/2017 [online]. Available at: https://www.walesonline.co.uk/sport/rugby/rugby-news/we-heading-car-crash-regional-12400972 [Accessed 28 August 2023].
8. Thomas, S., 'The radical proposal being discussed that will change Welsh rugby forever amid biggest shake-up in more than a decade', 6/1/2017 [online]. Available at: https://www.walesonline.co.uk/sport/rugby/rugby-news/radical-proposal-being-discussed-change-12415271 [Accessed 28 August 2023].
9. Dai Sport, 'Davies: "Modernisation One of the Most Significant Moments in WRU's 130-year History"', 14/10/2018 [online]. Available at: https://www.dai-sport.com/davies-wru-modernisation-history-agm/ [Accessed 27 August 2023].
10. Davies, G., in conversation with the author, 2023.
11. Jones, R., in conversation with the author, 2023.
12. Davies, G., in conversation with the author, 2023.

13. Williams, S., 'No. No. I just don't understand any more', Gwladrugby, 6/3/2019 [online]. Available at: https://gwladrugby. wordpress.com/2019/03/06/no-no-i-just-dont-understand-anymore/ [Accessed 28 August 2023].
14. Thomas, S., 'This is exactly how much each Welsh region receives in funding and why the Ospreys and Scarlets get more', Wales Online, 2/7/2019 [online]. Available at: https://www. walesonline.co.uk/sport/rugby/rugby-news/exactly-how-mucheach-welsh-16514855 [Accessed 28 August 2023].
15. Gatland, W., *Pride and Passion* (Headline, 2019), p.363.
16. Rees, P., 'Rob Howley banned from rugby for 18 months after placing bets on Wales', *The Guardian*, 16/12/2019 [online]. Available at: https://www.theguardian.com/sport/2019/dec/16/ wales-rob-howley-banned-18-months-rugby-betting#:~:text=The %20details%20of%20the%20charge,in%20your%20name%2C%2 0and%20received [Accessed 28 August 2023].

Chapter 9: Pandemic and Penury

1. BBC Sport, 'Amanda Blanc: Former Welsh Rugby Union board member discusses experience of misogyny', 12/3/2023 [online]. Available at: https://www.bbc.co.uk/sport/rugby-union/64917827 [Accessed 28 August 2023].
2. Thomas, S., 'One year on, the untold story of the Wales v Scotland game that was hours away from becoming a potentially catastrophic mistake', Wales Online, 12/3/2021 [online]. Available at: https://www.walesonline.co.uk/sport/rugby/rugbynews/one-year-on-untold-story-20057646 [Accessed 28 August 2023].
3. Evans, I. and Jackson, P., *Bread of Heaven* (Mainstream, 1998), pp.69, 209.
4. Thomas, S., '"My Rivals Will Ruin Welsh Rugby", Claims WRU Chief Gareth Davies In Leaked Letter Last Ditch Election Bid', Dai Sport, 11/9/2020 [online]. Available at: https://www.dai-sport. com/gareth-davies-welsh-rugby-union/ [Accessed 28 August 2023].
5. Jones, R., in conversation with the author, 2023.
6. Barry, S., 'Former Cardiff Blues chairman Peter Thomas writes off millions in loans to the club', Business Live, 5/2/2020 [online]. Available at: https://www.business-live.co.uk/professionalservices/banking-finance/former-cardiff-blues-chairman-peter-17681315.amp [Accessed 28 August 2023].

7. Jones, H., in conversation with the author, 2023.

8. Southcombe, M., '"I'm really worried about Wales as a rugby nation" – English rugby boss stunned by WRU's "inexplicable" loan', Wales Online, 12/10/2021 [online]. Available at: https://www.walesonline.co.uk/sport/rugby/rugby-news/im-really-worried-wales-rugby-21831866 [Accessed 28 August 2023].

9. Orders, M., 'Shane Williams claims WRU "actively work against the viability of the four regions" amid All Blacks controversy', Wales Online, 18/10/2021 [online]. Available at: https://www.walesonline.co.uk/sport/rugby/rugby-news/shane-williams-claims-wru-actively-21894499 [Accessed 28 August 2023].

10. Gulliver, B., 'Principality Stadium to get skywalk and zip wire attraction as plans approved', Wales Online, 25/11/2020 [online]. Available at: https://www.walesonline.co.uk/whats-on/whats-on-news/skywalk-cardiff-principality-stadium-zipwire-19346139 [Accessed 28 August 2023].

11. WRU, 'Women's Performance Rugby – Mid Term Strategy Review – Recommendations, July 2021', 31/1/2023 [online]. Available at: https://business.senedd.wales/documents/s137355/Welsh%20Rugby%20Union%20Womens%20Performance%20Rugby%20-%20Mid%20Term%20Strategy%20Review%20Recommendations%20-%20July%202021.pdf [Accessed 2 September 2023].

12. Barnes, S., 'Unhealthy obsession with the national team is killing Welsh rugby', *The Times*, 5/5/2022 [online]. Available at: https://www.thetimes.co.uk/article/unhealthy-obsession-with-the-national-team-is-killing-welsh-rugby-swl62nxm9 [Accessed 28 August 2023].

13. Southcombe, M., 'How to save Welsh rugby – The uncomfortable truth facing our game and the difficult solutions that need to be explored', Wales Online, 12/4/2022 [online]. Available at: https://www.walesonline.co.uk/sport/rugby/rugby-news/how-save-welsh-rugby-uncomfortable-23671119 [Accessed 28 August 2023].

14. Thomas, S., 'David Moffett: There is enough money for only three Welsh sides – WRU-owned Dragons should be cut', *The Times*, 6/5/2022 [online]. Available at: https://www.thetimes.co.uk/article/david-moffett-there-is-enough-money-for-only-three-welsh-sides-wru-owned-dragons-should-be-cut-k5vsshsxc [Accessed 28 August 2023].

15. Thomas, S., 'WRU Tell Regions: "Here's £30m For Your Players… It's Mostly A Loan, And Your Money Men Have To Carry The Risk"', Dai Sport, 4/9/2022 [online]. Available at:

https://www.dai-sport.com/wru-tell-regions-heres-30m-for-your-players-its-mostly-a-loan-and-your-money-men-have-to-carry-the-risk/ [Accessed 28 August 2023].

16. Thomas, S., 'Scarlets boss warns "one or more" regions won't survive as he goes public in attack on Welsh rugby madhouse', Wales Online, 22/12/2022 [online]. Available at: https://www.walesonline.co.uk/sport/rugby/rugby-news/scarlets-boss-warns-one-more-25814131 [Accessed 27 August 2023].

17. BBC Sport, 'Amanda Blanc: Former Welsh Rugby Union board member discusses experience of misogyny', 12/3/2023 [online]. Available at: https://www.bbc.co.uk/sport/rugby-union/64917827 [Accessed 28 August 2023].

18. Bywater, A., 'Cardiff director Hayley Parsons says Welsh Rugby is "fundamentally broken from top to bottom" after allegations of sexism and misogyny… as she adds to calls for WRU chief executive Steve Phillips to resign from his position', *Daily Mail*, 26/1/2023 [online]. Available at: https://www.dailymail.co.uk/sport/rugbyunion/article-11680875/Cardiff-director-says-Welsh-Rugby-broken-bottom-sexism-misogyny-claims.html?ico=authors_pagination_desktop [Accessed 28 August 2023].

19. Jones, R., in conversation with the author, 2023.

20. Bywater, A., in conversation with the author, 2023.

Chapter 10: The Road to Redemption?

1. Liew, J., 'Strike threats and Netflix feuds: Wales's rugby crisis exposes greater problem', *The Guardian*, 20/2/2023 [online]. Available at: https://www.theguardian.com/sport/blog/2023/feb/20/strike-threats-netflix-feuds-wales-rugby-union-crisis [Accessed 27 August 2023].

2. Bywater, A., '"Young men are sometimes a little bit impulsive": Wales coach Warren Gatland rebukes his team over strike threat… now he must fire them up for Six Nations clash against England', *Daily Mail*, 23/2/2023 [online]. Available at: https://www.dailymail.co.uk/sport/rugbyunion/article-11786491/Wales-coach-Gatland-rebukes-team-strike-threat-fire-England.html?ico=authors_pagination_desktop [Accessed 27 August 2023].

3. Jones, H., in conversation with the author, 2023.

4. Williams, C., Evans, N. and O'Leary, P., *A Tolerant Nation?: Exploring Ethnic Diversity in Wales* (2003).

5. Johnes, M., *A History of Sport in Wales* (University of Wales Press, 2005), p.103.
6. Maguire, J., 'Sport, identity politics, and globalization: diminishing contrasts and increasing varieties', *Sociology of Sport Journal*, 11:4 (1994), p.412, quoted in Johnes, M., *A History of Sport in Wales* (University of Wales Press, 2005), p.110.
7. WRU, 'Walker publishes details of 2021 Women's Performance Mid-term review', 15/6/2023 [online]. Available at: https://www.wru.wales/2023/06/walker-publishes-details-of-2021-womens-performance-mid-term-review/ [Accessed 23 October 2023].
8. Bywater, A., in conversation with the author, 2023.
9. Richards, H., 'Welsh Rugby Comment: What are the Welsh regions for?', ESPN Scrum, 24/7/2013 [online]. Available at: http://en.espn.co.uk/wales/rugby/story/191889.html [Accessed 27 August 2023].
10. Bishop, N. and Carter, A., *The Good, The Bad and The Ugly – The Rise and Fall of Pontypool RFC* (Random House, 2013), p.238.
11. Figures drawn from https://cardiffrfcfans.com.
12. Thomas, S., 'Grand Slam skipper warns Welsh rugby is built on sand as he issues scathing assessment and calls for radical change', Wales Online, 3/8/2020. Available at: https://www.walesonline.co.uk/sport/rugby/rugby-news/grand-slam-skipper-warns-welsh-18706423 [Accessed 24 October 2023].
13. Jones, R., in conversation with the author, 2023.
14. Jones, H., in conversation with the author, 2023.
15. Stead, P. and Richards, H., 'At The Millennium', in Richards, H., Stead, P. and Williams, G., *More Heart and Soul* (1999), p.5.

Acknowledgements

THIS BOOK IS written from the perspective, not of a player or coach or journalist, but of a lifelong supporter of the game. I am grateful to all at Y Lolfa for commissioning and leading me through its production, especially Lefi, Eirian and Alan, to Sion Ilar for the cover, and to Cyngor Llyfrau Cymru for their support. My thanks to David, Kelvin, Dan and Phil for their advice, fact-checking and proofreading, and to everybody who agreed to speak to me on and off the record. Special thanks to Stephen Jones for his Foreword. Thank you also to all Gwladers, past and present, for the campaigning, the arguments, the socials, the arguments and the laughs. But mainly the arguments. And most importantly, thank you to my family for their endless patience while I disappeared into my shed to write this.